What People are Saying

Jim Spears (Attorney, Public Defender and former Judge) assembles his case, gathers overwhelming evidence, and consults a long line of witnesses to set the record straight on the Cuban Refugees at Fort Chaffee, a forgotten and misunderstood story that cast Fort Smith in the national spotlight, involved the Ku Klux Klan, almost cost William Jefferson Clinton his political career, and contributed to President Carter's defeat by Ronald Reagan.

Tom Wing, Professor of History, UAFS

* * *

Yearning to Breathe reads like a novel, but this story really happened. Jim Spears' research is impeccable, and the compelling stories he tells are enriched with first person quotes. The photographs are poignant, breathing empathy into this largely forgotten chapter in our history. Stories like this should not be lost, and Judge Spears has done yeoman's work in making sure we remember a time when anxiety was high and fear of an onslaught of mostly unwelcome immigrants, was acute.

Larry Foley, Chair
University of Arkansas School of Journalism
Documentary filmmaker

* * *

A timely book based on primary sources, historical photographs, and personal accounts, including his own, legal expert Jim Spears' detailed and sensitive account of the embattled Mariel refugees kept at Fort Chaffee in the early 1980's will find a prominent place on many book shelves including my own. Don't miss reading Chapter IX, "Atticus Finch Redux!"

Billy D. Higgins, author of *Navigating the C-124 Globemaster: In the Cockpit of America's First Heavylifter.*

YEARNING

TO

BREATHE

FREE
A JUDICIAL HISTORY OF THE
CUBAN RELOCATION PROJECT
FORT CHAFFEE, ARKANSAS
1980-82

JUDGE JIM SPEARS

Library of Congress Control Number:2019942326

ISBN: 978-1-943267-69-9-paperback

Cover Art by Joyce Faulkner

Printed in the United States.

Red Engine Press

To all those people who bravely set out for a new life in a strange land and have made America great. The name may have been Annie Moore, the first person to be processed through Ellis Island, or Anna Morales, a refugee from Guatemala seeking asylum at the southern border. It most certainly is the young man whose daughter was ripped from his arms as he sought shelter in the Peruvian Embassy in his quest for freedom.

FOREWORD

THIS IS AN ATTEMPT to record a special time in the history of our area. A time when we were singled out to handle a situation that no one asked for but could not be avoided. All were not happy and some very angry.

It was a different time and place than today. It was a time when we took the Emma Lazarus poem, "The New Colossus" seriously. One might recall this penned for the dedication of the Statue of Liberty in New York Harbor. It read:

Not like the brazen giant of Greek fame,
With conquering limbs astride from land to land;
Here at our sea-washed, sunset gates shall stand,
A mighty woman with a torch, whose flame
Is the imprisoned lightning and her name is Mother of Exiles.
From her beacon-hand
Glows world-wide welcome; her mild eyes command,
The air-bridged harbor that twin cities frame,
"Keep, ancient lands, your storied pomp!" cries she with silent lips.
"Give me your tired, your poor,
Your huddled masses yearning to breathe free,
The wretched refuse of your teeming shore,
Send these, the homeless, tempest-tost to me,
I lift my lamp beside the golden door!

In May of 1980, this was put to the test and the United States and Fort Smith, Arkansas passed with flying colors—notwithstanding the fears that accompany new and strange-to-us people in our midst. Many of them were ill mentally and physically. Some were criminals and misfits. In retrospect and being conscious of the present leadership and attitudes, I wonder what our reaction as a nation and community would be today. We have leaders now who would build walls and take children from parents that are merely seeking asylum from drug gangs and human trafficking. Racism, by such groups as the KKK, rejected and laughed at in Fort Smith in 1980, is having a resurgence. It is fear of the future and a changing world. But there was a time when we were not afraid and we were truly a great nation.

In compiling this I relied almost exclusively on the reporters of the *Southwest Times Record*, the daily paper serving the people of western Arkansas and eastern Oklahoma for many years. The news business was different then and this was a class news organization. There was no CNN or MSNBC or Fox News in those days. Local broadcasts and newspapers were where we got information. It has been said that the newspapers are the first edit of history. This is a fine edition! I am unaware if the SWTR won a Pulitzer for their coverage but they should have. The reporting was excellent and the editorials helped keep the situation in hand. I give a special shout-out to my friend Jack Moseley who was the editor of the SWTR in those days.

I want to give special thanks to my friends Professor Tom Wing and Lynn Wasson for their help and suggestions.

Jim D. Spears
July 24, 2018

Cubans Arrive In Fort Smith

I

THE BOATLIFT

IN APRIL OF 1980, Jimmy Carter was president and Bill Clinton was governor of Arkansas. Events about to unfold would play a big roll in neither being reelected for a second term.

First, the economy in Cuba tanked. When the Cuban people began seeking asylum in various South American embassies, the stage was set for what became the Mariel Boat Lift.1 The unsuspecting little city of Fort Smith, Arkansas would feel its effects.

It all began in January of that year when some Cubans crashed a bus through a fence at the Venezuelan embassy in Havana and crowded inside. Others flocked to the Peruvian embassy. One man in the crowd carried his young daughter in his arms as he tried to get into the Peruvian embassy. The Cuban police, armed with clubs, beat them. As he fell to the ground, they pulled his daughter away from him He turned to search for her but, using their clubs, the police pushed him out and locked the embassy doors behind him. He was left only with a photograph and no idea as to the fate of his daughter.2

---

1   Mariel boatlift, in Wikpedia, 8-22-2016
2   *Southwest Times Record* vol. 90 # 139, May 18, 1980

On April 4, after months of confrontation, the Cuban authorities withdrew their security forces and announced that anyone who had come to the embassies were free to leave—provided another country would accept them. By nightfall on April 5, over two thousand persons were inside the Peruvian embassy. By the next day it was ten thousand.[3] On April 16, an airlift carried eleven thousand Cubans to San Jose, Costa Rica, which acted as a staging area for transport to other countries. The United States agreed to accept thirty-five hundred of these displaced persons.[4] No one anticipated what was to happen.

As the dissident Cubans prepared to board planes bound for Costa Rica, soldiers took their personal belongings from them including money and other valuables. They left with merely the clothes on their backs.[5] They even pulled a ninety-six-year-old man's gold teeth.[6]

These people wanted to go to Miami and the various other countries that agreed to take them in. This Fidel Castro knew. Relishing the trouble his act would cause the United States, he ended the flights to Costa Rica.[7]

When the flights stopped, a boatlift began. All the refugees would have to go to the United States—specifically Florida. The *Associated Press* story headlined:

Refugees Head for U.S.; Cubans Man Boats. Mariel, Cuba.

Boats manned by Cuban exiles in Florida headed for the U. S. with more than 200 refugees from the Peruvian embassy in Havana aboard. Twenty more boats were in Mariel Harbor and more

3   Wikipedia, ibid
4   *Southwest Times Record*, vol. 86 # 107, April 16, 1980
5   *Southwest Times Record*, vol. 86 # 109, April 18, 1980
6   *Southwest Times Record*, vol. 86 # 139, May 18, 1980
7   Wikipedia, ibid

than 300 boats were authorized to leave by the Cuban government.

This was a private mission by hundreds of Cuban expatriates living in Florida. One shrimp boat carried two-hundred-and-fifteen people. To complicate things a spokesman for the U.S. State Department said, "This is not in accordance with U.S. policy and bringing illegal aliens into the country is a felony."[8]

"Cubans Bring Boom to Town" was the newspaper headline referring to Key West. The ten-thousand-Cuban exiles in Florida were anxious to liberate their loved ones in Cuba. Napoleon Villaboa, a spokesman for the "Freedom Flotilla" and its organizer, said, "Castro has opened the doors."

More than three hundred boats crowded into Mariel Harbor. Boats in Florida were sold for more than twice their value in order to aid in the project. Some boat captains charged one thousand dollars per refugee for the transit—and the store shelves in Key West were empty. There was not a life vest or fire extinguisher to be found. One shrimp boat captain grossed one-hundred-and-seventy-thousand dollars on Sunday.[9]

The trip was horrific. Jose Rogue, a refugee interviewed at Fort Chaffee, said that death would have been preferable. "If I would have thought of it twice, I would have decided to die instead." He decided to leave after suffering political and physical harassment. Cuban officials came to his house on Monday and asked him if he wanted to leave the country. When he agreed, they put him in a facility at Mariel Bay that resembled a Nazi concentration camp. There the crisis began. No food. The water was hot. One hundred people crowded into the army tents where they were searched and robbed. They had no idea what was going to happen to them.

---

8 *Southwest Times Record*, vol. 86 #114 April 23, 1980 (AP story)
9 Ibid, # 119, April 29, 1980, (AP story)

Rogue ended up on a shrimp boat along with three hundred other refugees. The trip was a nightmare. Eighteen hours at sea in stormy weather. Many became sea sick. He feared drowning.

Rogue said that the boat captain paid the Cuban government twenty-five thousand dollars for the right to come to Cuba to search for relatives. When he could not find them, he took three hundred others instead.[10]

Some boats broke down in the stormy seas. The U.S. Coast Guard rescued them. Florida Governor Bob Graham declared an emergency and called out the National Guard due to hurricane-force winds. By April 30, the winds had calmed and a new wave of refugees made it to the shores of Florida. Meanwhile, twelve-hundred and fifty boats at Mariel took on even more displaced persons for the next transit.

Key West officials reported that more than two-thousand boats had been launched and more than thirteen-hundred persons made the voyage during the first week. Mr. Villaboa, the spokesman, expected that more than two-hundred-and-fifty-thousand Cubans might leave the island. It was chaotic. No one knew what was going to happen next. The average age of the exiles was around twenty and ominously, some of the refugees reported that many of their number were criminals and misfits. "Castro is sending his 'incorrigibles,'" they said. About that time the stream slowed and some wondered if Castro had changed his mind. Then Cuban troops, along with Russians, showed up on shore and the pace quickened again.[111213]

Governor Bob Graham encouraged the Carter administration to continue seizing the boats as the passage was extremely dangerous. To avoid seizure, some of the

10 Kevin Laval, *Southwest Times Record*, vol. 86 # 132, May 11, 1980
11 *Southwest Times Record*, vol. 86 # 114, April 23, 1980 (AP story)
12 Ibid, # 119, April 29, 1980
13 Ibid, # 121, April 30, 1980

captains off-loaded their passengers near beaches where they swam or walked to dry land.

President Carter ordered the U.S. Navy to assist these "boat people." Ships, diverted from maneuvers, helped during the emergency. The plan was to airlift these people to processing centers in order to screen out criminals, reunite families and otherwise resettle the new arrivals.[14]

Evacuation flights began from Key West to Eglin AFB near Pensacola. A tent city housed them. The population grew by twelve hundred persons per day. By this time, thirteen-thousand people had made it to Key West since Castro opened the port at Mariel. Four persons drowned and one lady suffered a heart attack upon reaching the U. S. It was a treacherous undertaking.[15]

On May 6, President Carter vowed to accept Cuban refugees. He stated in a speech:

The U. S. will welcome these Cuban refugees with open arms. The U.S. is the most generous nation on earth in receiving refugees and I feel very deeply that this commitment should be maintained.

More people continued to arrive. A political cartoon mimicking the old Uncle Sam needs you recruiting poster made the rounds. It was Castro pointing to the front and saying, "Who needs you."[16]

On May 7, the Federal government, at the request of Governor Bob Graham, declared a state of emergency in Florida due to the eighteen thousand Cubans in the state. Supplies of food and clothing ran short. Concerns of criminality within the masses seeking refuge slowed the screening process. One immigration officer stated, "These people aren't immigrating, they are being

14   Ibid, # 122, April 31, 1980
15   Ibid, # 126, May 5, 1980
16   Ibid, # 127, May 6, 1980

deported." Many of them were guilty of minor offenses or had been political prisoners. According to U.S. Marshal Driscoll O'Glesby, the U.S. Marshals Service took sixty-two persons, single males from teenage to their thirties, into custody and transported them to the Federal prison at Talledega. Determined to be a threat to the people of the United States, they were held for violation of immigration laws and offenses committed in Cuba ranging from simple assault to murder.[17]

LOCAL OPINIONS

---

17   Ibid, # 128, May 7, 1980

II

Twenty-two Days in May

ON MAY 8, 1980, the headline in the *Southwest Times Record* in Fort Smith read: "Chaffee to House Cuban Refugees." As thousands of Indochinese refugees reflected on the 5th anniversary of their passage through Chaffee in 1975, the aging Army base would once again open its gates to a flood of refugees, this time from Cuba. The tent city at Eglin AFB could no longer handle the numbers of people crowded inside. Congressman John Paul Hammerschmidt had been notified, but the announcement caught the officers in charge of Fort Chaffee by surprise. There had been speculation but the public affairs officers on base had no notice until news agencies began to call. They refused any questions until they got official notification. They later advised that the first refugees would be arriving as soon as the weekend. The goal was to have the base fully operational within a week.

The plan, obviously devised on the fly, was to receive as many as twelve-hundred persons per day.

Chaffee was only to be a holding facility after processing was completed in Florida. The Cubans were then to be connected with sponsors and moved out. This was to prove not to be the case. It was also unknown as to how much assistance the skeleton crew then at Chaffee, numbering three-hundred and sixty-four civilians and military, would receive. There was a public affairs information detachment from Fort Hood, Texas on its way to deal with the press. The military spokesman thought that five or six days would be needed to get ready for the refugees but that the Army would make due. It was also suggested that the arrival of additional personnel and refugees would not interfere with scheduled National Guard training programs. That would prove to be wishful thinking. [1]

Richard Burford, who ran a beer distributorship in Fort Smith, had lived fifteen years in Cuba and owned a sugar plantation and cattle operation that had been seized by the Castro government after the revolution. Burford opined at the time that the influx of Cuban refugees would be detrimental to both countries. It would strengthen the Cuban's political power in FL and the U.S. and weaken opposition to Castro in Cuba. "It is not going to help the Cuban cause one bit." he stated. "I don't think any of them would ever be interested in settling in Fort Smith. They would seek a Cuban-like environment in South Florida." This is where many of the Cubans fleeing Castro following the revolution ended up.

Burford's father and mother had settled in Cuba in 1898, following the Spanish American War. They thought that Cuba would become a U.S. possession. Burford returned there in 1947, after buying his father's sugar plantation and cattle ranch. He was a friend of Fulgencio Batista the Cuban leader later deposed by Fidel Castro. Burford related that the Cubans that came here in the 1960s were much different. "They were doctors, lawyers, accountants and very educated." He also stated that the ones coming now would all go to Florida because, "They are as clannish as they can be." He was concerned about the political power the newcomers

1   Ray Robinson, *Southwest Times Record*, vol. 86 #129, May 8, 1980

would give the Cuban community. "If they are going to have political clout they should have used it in Cuba. "Letting them in was a mistake but we need to make the best of it and learn from their bad experiences," he opined. It seems that Mr. Burford had a lot of insight into the Cuban people as evidenced by today's political landscape in Florida.[2]

Economics were on the mind of most area residents. "Fort Smith will have the same reaction as it did for the Vietnamese. The people here have proven they can rise to the occasion. It should be a big relief to the unemployment situation," stated Frances Witeler.

A farmer from Poteau disagreed, "I'm definitely not in favor of them coming. America should send all of them (immigrants) back but the Americans, the Indians and the Negros. They'll just get here and the government'll tax us people more to give them houses...."

Roy Chessmore, also of Poteau said, "It's going to be hard on the local labor force I'm afraid....I expect the Cubans to be like many of the Vietnamese who have stayed in the area and are good workers."

Alma Armbruster of Ratcliff stated, "We should be compassionate but I think there should be a limit (referring to the acceptance of the Vietnamese) I really have mixed feelings about it."

Nancy Kleck of Fort Smith stated, "We should take care of our own people first. There are enough people to feed already. It could take away employment from our own people."

Dale Rogers of Fort Smith echoed Ms. Armbruster when he stated, "But there already aren't enough jobs."

Stephanie Rhodes age fourteen: "These people don't have any place else to live. I don't think it is wrong to help them."

2   Kevin Laval, Ibid

Tony Kendig, age eighteen from Alma: "I feel just the opposite. I don't think they should be here or we Americans picking up the tab. I think there could be some spies in the group and from what I have heard they are that country's rejects."

Ralph Coleman opined, "People have been talking about it all afternoon. The people who are knowledgeable about the Vietnamese situation are favorable to the Cuban possibility. They think it will have the same effect of providing jobs and enhancing Fort Smith's image nationally."

Paul Wester of Fort Smith: "The only thing that bothers me is there is only a certain number of jobs. What about the jobs that fifteen-thousand American people need? And now with the unemployment rate going up and Whirlpool and Rheem laying off it's just a bad time. But accepting these people is the kind-hearted American philosophy."

Earl Howard, the manager of the Trade Winds hotel: "This is just a shot in the arm for Fort Smith. I know it will help my business and put a lot of unemployed people to work."

Many interviewed by the paper did not want to be quoted but agreed with a young black nurse who stated, "The government is going to send them here whatever I think."[3]

The congressional delegation took a calm approach. Senator Dale Bumpers stated that he did not want Fort Chaffee to become another Ellis Island. Senator David Pryor, who was governor during the Vietnamese migration, said this would be different. "The Vietnamese had financial resources the Cubans don't have and some are known criminals."[4]

---

3 Debbye Hughes, *Southwest Times Record*, vol. 86 #129 May 8, 1980
4 Terry Wade, Ibid

"First Cubans to Arrive Saturday," was the headline on May 8. The press was told that up to twenty-thousand refugees could be coming to Chaffee and that the first plane of Cubans would be arriving after 3 p.m, Friday, May 9, not Saturday. These were to be followed by another planeload four hours later. It had begun.

Support military personnel would also be arriving. FEMA coordinated the airlift, the City of Fort Smith provided airport security and standby fire Protection. And Immigration and Naturalization Service handled processing. To house the refugees, Chaffee renovated one hundred and forty-two barracks, adding partitions for privacy. The preparations included recreational facilities, food service, and laundries. Spokesmen for these organizations assured reporters that local people would be involved in providing these services. Five hundred persons were expected to arrive the first day and two thousand per day in the future.[5]

On May 10, the *Southwest Time Register* headline read:

Cubans Land Shouting 'Freedom.'

Waving at a crowd of reporters and shouting "Viva America!" and "Freedom!" the first planeload of Cubans landed Friday May 9, at the Ft. Smith Municipal Airport after 6 pm. 128 men clutching plastic Red Cross bags containing shaving equipment descended onto the tarmac. The first refugee off the plane had to be assisted by two soldiers, one on each arm. Many shouted, "Down With Castro' and "Up With Carter" "Viva Carter." One asked for a trumpet so he could play the Star Spangled Banner which he had practiced since he was a little boy. Another plane brought the next load at about 11pm.

5   Joanne Norton, *Southwest Times Record*, vol. 86 # 129, May 8, 1980

While they were waiting on the tarmac, a man wearing a white robe and a pointed hat ran at them screaming, "Don't let the Cubans in! Stop the Cubans! Carter's letting in all these Cubans and foreigners!" Claiming to represent a group called SCAT, he identified himself as Mack McCarty of Leslie and said he was a retired Marine. Buddy Acoach, a state trooper and member of the guard along with Officer Larry Hammond FSPD, also a guard member, arrested McCarty and stripped him of his robes. He was later released but he vowed to return. Otherwise the welcome of the refugees seemed warm.

It turned out the Cuban refugees had only rudimentary processing in Florida contrary to what was earlier announced. They had not been screened for health problems or criminal activity. They were quickly processed for the night and billeted at the fort. There were rolls of razor wire around the buildings and MPs guarded several blocks. One Cuban, when asked why he made the trip said that he had a brother, sister and a son in New York City. Lazora Ruiz Romero, age thirty, said he had been sentenced to prison at age sixteen for sabotage. Others proclaimed, "This is the Mother State of Liberty, not only for Cubans, it is the Mother State for all countries."[6]

Within twenty-four hours, the original processing schedule had to be scrapped as preliminary assessments in Florida had not occurred. There were many reasons for this. For example, many dialects are spoken in Cuba. Someone from other countries, as were most translators, had a difficult time communicating with these refugees. As a result, it could take up to four hours to process a single person.

There were also more refugees than expected. The planners hoped that the first group would leave the base

---

6   *Southwest Times Record*, vol 86 #131, May 10, 1980 (AP story)

by the next Tuesday since the full compliment of twenty-thousand was to arrive by May 18.

The refugees were happy and cooperative, lounging around the barracks and playing catch. Reporters interviewed three Cubans including a convict who robbed a man of a watch, a black market clothing dealer and a chemist who was a political prisoner.[7]

The next day, four persons appeared at the front gate of Fort Chaffee with signs. Sheryl Phelps of Fort Smith said, "We don't have room for them." Her sign read, "Go Home Cubans, We've Got Enough Foreigners Over Here Now." These Arkansans were concerned that the Cubans would take American jobs and that there might be Communist agents among them.

"This is our country. We belong here. I just think they should be over there. We don't want to be prejudiced against these people but we just don't want them here. We just want what is right," stated Bettye Hughes of Arkoma. Her sign read, "God Keep America Free." She went on to explain her fears. "This is part of Castro's strategy. He has something in mind. They can't be trusted. No, I don't believe their reason for coming over here. I don't believe they've changed American. In one way or another their Communist's beliefs."

Several passing motorists expressed their support. "Tell the American people to speak up while we still have freedom of speech. There are Cubans invading America with our eyes open," Hughes concluded.[8]

The 47th Field Hospital detachment was set up to provide medical care. They performed medical screenings. They found people with colds, thyroid disease, diabetes, fevers and dehydration—as well as two pregnant women. All had to be treated at the field hospital.

7   Ray Robinson, *Southwest Times Record*, vol. 86 # 132, May 11, 1980
8   Kevin Laval, *Southwest Times Record*, vol. 86 #132, May 11, 1980

Volunteer agencies worked to resettle people. Sixty percent of the refugees named family members living in the U.S. These relatives were contacted to see if arrangements could be worked out.[9]

By Monday, the community of displaced Cubans began to assume an identity. Catholic and Protestant church services were available—as well as a Spanish language newspaper, "La Nuevo Vida" or "The New Life."[10]

The Lord said unto Moses, 'Go in unto Pharoah and tell him; Thus says the Lord God of the Hebrews, Let My People Go that they may serve me.

This was the theme the first religious service many of the Cubans, who were predominately Catholic, had attended in many years. It compared them to the Hebrews coming out of Egypt during the Exodus. Brother Francis Marin delivered the homily and Father Jerome Kodel performed the mass. They both were from Subiaco Monastery.

Brother Marin was fluent in Spanish. With his family, he fled Cuba in 1960 when Castro took over. An army soldier present at the mass related that as an infant with his family, he escaped to Puerto Rico. He was bitter toward the Castro regime. "This is our Holocaust," he stated.[11]

A sixteen-year-old girl named Elaine Zar who had no family or friends in the U.S. showed the optimism of some of the Cubans. She had no marketable skills. The other Cubans staying in the barracks with her were her surrogate family. "Here we get all the food we want," she bragged. She wanted to go to New York City. "Down there (Cuba) they treat us bad, the people are just happy here."

9 Joanne Norton, Ibid
10 Kevin Laval, *Southwest Times Record*, vol. 86 # 133, May 12, 1980
11 Joanne Norton, Ibid

The numbers of refugees arriving in Florida surpassed what could be handled at Chaffee. In order to deal with the overflow, the government set up other relocation centers at Fort Indian Town Gap in Pennsylvania and Bainbridge Naval Training Center near Baltimore, Maryland.[12]

The impact of the relocation operation on the local economy was evident. Officials at Chaffee purchased thirty-one thousand half-pint-milk cartons from Foremost Dairy and nineteen-thousand and eight-hundred half pints from Acee Dairy daily. The center also purchased athletic equipment and handed it out to the Cubans. They hired local people to support the camp— and government workers stayed in area hotels and ate at nearby restaurants.

Unfortunately not all were happy that the Cubans were here. The KKK planned a protest. Candy Howard of Rogers received permission from base commander Colonel Ray Spence to march near the main gate with about twelve others. She stated:

We'll conduct ourselves like white people...They are all communist or pro-communist. These Cubans, if they were truly anti-communist, they wouldn't have asked for clothes and cars and homes and jobs when they got here; they would have asked for guns to fight Castro![13]

---

12   Kevin Laval, Ibid
13   *Southwest Times Record*, vol. 86 # 135, May 14, 1980 (AP story)

OUTSIDE AGITATORS

All was not well among the refugees. Three were in custody for attempting to stir up a protest against America. However, two hundred anti-Castro Cubans armed themselves with sticks and rocks and appeared ready to kill the trio. The MPs moved in. One observer said:

The two hundred refugees from the same section in the compound wanted to strip them naked, slit their throats and parade them up and down the barricade to show the American people how grateful they are to be here.

U.S. Marshals arrested the three and placed them in the Sebastian County jail.[14]

The base moved from activation to a sustaining phase. Gossip abounded. Rumors that two Cuban girls escaped were not true. It was a simple domestic dispute. Stories about a tuberculosis outbreak among the Cubans was also incorrect. Five questionable spots had shown up on x-ray but there were no confirmed cases of TB. The same was true of sexually transmitted disease. There were only two visual confirmations of syphilis out of seven hundred and fifty screenings. Hearsay had

14   Jack Moseley, Ibid

it that 60% were mentally ill. Not so, only one case was admitted to the mental health unit at St. Edward hospital. Perhaps anxiety and apprehension were misinterpreted as more serious problems.

In the meantime money flowed into the local economy. People got jobs—and Spanish speakers were in high demand.

On a different level, the Carter administration worked to stem the flow of additional refugees. They threated boat captains with heavy fines and jail. Even though vessels were seized, the total number of Cubans coming through Florida was now over forty-five-thousand (45,000.) The Treasury Department announced that anyone convicted of helping Cubans come here illegally could be subject to a $50,000 fine and ten years in prison. President Carter said that the U.S. could not be used as a dumping ground for Cuba's criminals and refugees. He also noted that the ragtag boatlift was too dangerous and that no more boats would be permitted to leave Florida—and those in Mariel must return empty.

The official Cuban newspaper, "Granma," opined, "Carter governs in Florida, but in Mariel, Cuba governs!" They went on to explain that Cuba would not interfere with any boat captain that wants to take Cubans to Florida. So it continued.[15]

And so, refugees continued to arrive at Fort Chaffee. Although no suspected criminals had been identified in the screening process, problems began to arise. This is to be expected when there are large numbers of people in a limited space with little to do. The disturbances were mostly in the mess hall. One woman had a nine-inch-long and one-half-inch-deep slash across her chest inflicted by her boyfriend. He used a razor blade taken from a shaving kit given to the refugees. He was arrested in the barracks and taken to the county jail.

15   Joanne Norton, *Southwest Times Record*, vol. 86 #137, May 16, 1980

The incident resulted in the first criminal charge filed against a refugee for activity in the compound.

U.S. Attorney Larry McCord charged Juan Borrass Boiz, age twenty-two, with assault. Filed with U.S. Magistrate Ned Stewart, Jr., the case could have resulted in a $500 fine and up to six months in jail. No one knew exactly where he would serve his time if convicted. It turned out he was sentenced to twenty days in jail with credit for time served—and spent the remaining fourteen days in the Sebastian County jail. Chief Deputy U.S. Marshal Jim Smith advised he would be presenting more cases to the U.S. Attorney in the near future.[16]

To help refugees adapt to life in the compound and this country, they were provided English lessons and recreational opportunities. The government supplied them with a boxing ring, soccer and baseball equipment. The refugees especially enjoyed boxing despite the harsh sun and sultry air. The portable canvas ring was set up between barracks buildings in a field—and boxers of all sizes and shapes competed. To better regulate the events by the size of the competitors, the authorities even authorized the purchase of a scale.

FEMA hired Wesley Parker and Harold Lassiter to manage the recreational center. "They are great to work with, no trouble at all," said Parker. The refugees also enjoyed volleyball, soccer, flag football and the most popular of all, softball. Several officials noted that the Cubans had a natural talent for baseball.[17]

The military contingent also continued to grow. The army brought in Brigadier General James "Bulldog" Drummond, whose regular job was as commander of the 3rd Artillery Corps at Fort Sill, Oklahoma, as the operations commander at Fort Chaffee. Drummond related that only one soldier complained about the long

16   Southwest Times Record, vol. 86 # 135, May 14, 1980 (AP story)
17   Kevin Laval, *Southwest Times Record*, vol. 86 #138 May 17, 1980

18

hours and working conditions arising from the relocation project. He sent that man home. "We've got too
many people here who felt the emotional bond. I just
don't need a reluctant person." He further explained
that since the base was moving to the sustaining phase
of Operation, scheduling was more manageable. His
main concern the arrival of more and more refugees. He
complimented the support troops especially those first
on the scene to open the base. Although Spanish-speak-
ing troops were not trained interpreters, INS and FEMA
used them for that task.

*I have found in my association with them (the
refugees) that it is a fairly representative cut of
society. We've got the total spectrum down there.*

Photos of his children, Jim, a cadet at West Point,
and daughter Sarah who was soon graduate high school
in Lawton, adorned his office. "Her graduation is the
end of May; I wouldn't miss it for the world."[18] The
events that would come at the end of May raised doubts
as to whether he made it.

A lady with a crying baby being helped by a young
soldier emphasized the points made by General Drummond. Spec 4 David Sanchez held the young child while
the mother took her other children to the bathroom. He
continued to talk while holding the crying child. "He's
the kind of guy I would trade a battalion for." Drummond said.

Sanchez was a records specialist with the 545th Per-
sonal Service Complement when summoned to Chaffee.
His job was to welcome people as they got off the bus.
He did this for eighteen hours straight at first then less
as the groups of arrivals slackened and there were more
Spanish speaking interpreters. The Cubans liked him.

Sanchez said:

18   Joanne Norton, Southwest Times Record, vol. 86 # 139 May 18, 1980

I think it is the language, I'm from Puerto Rico and they are from Cuba. They have a feeling of warmness toward other Latin American countries. I'm here to cheer them up a little. A lot of them are going through a lot of trouble once they get out of here. I tell them, 'I know what you've been through. It is like when I came to America.

That was in 1976 and he could speak no English. He joined the army two years later with an expanding vocabulary.

"One of them brought a book, the same book I used to learn English," he commented. His job was to put them at ease and give them information. He used jokes and comforting comments:

You're going to get an ID card like this. It won't look as good as this because this is me in the picture!

This made the refugees laugh. Despite the long hours, each group was different.

I like to do it. It makes me feel good, doing something to help them out.[19]

By May 20, the population of Fort Chaffee reached nineteen thousand making it the eleventh-largest city in Arkansas. There were one-hundred-twenty unaccompanied children identified and segregated at Chaffee. They, most likely, went to a Roman Catholic orphanage. Agencies working to place refugees were the U.S. Catholic Conference, World Relief Organization, the International Refugee Committee, the Southern Baptist Convention and World Church Services.[20]

---

19   Joanne Norton, Southwest Times Record, vol. 86 #139, May 18, 1980
20   Joanne Norton, *Southwest Times Record*, vol. 86 # 140, May 19, 1980

There was an incident where some Cubans temporarily left the base and this became the focus of attention. Deputy Smith maintained that no one should be alarmed:

Sometimes their patience runs a little short. They are anxious to be reunited with their families.

This interview predated the headline, "30 refugees attempt to leave post." This was the front page.

Only eight succeeded in leaving post. The official version was that two were captured in Barling and six in downtown Fort Smith. They had started leaving in small groups over the weekend. The official total was increased to forty-five attempts with twenty-four being successful. The Sebastian County Sheriff's office said even more had been caught and returned. The base officials said those attempting to leave were only seeking cigarettes and posed no threat.

Security problems continued on the base. There were five thefts including footlockers containing up to fifteen knives. There were other thefts from dining halls along with some refugee's personal property. Dissatisfaction was growing among the detainees.[21]

There were two disturbances on post. The first, previously mentioned, was about two-hundred refugees pointing out one of their number as a spy. It worked and the man was taken into custody.

Another was over the attempted theft of a man's mattress. There was no violence against any American. But rumors of a mass escape attempt continued to multiply in the community despite the official line that the post was under control. Deputy Marshal Smith told of getting a call about five Cubans in a motel. It turned out to be a Cuban family from Florida who had come to pick up a relative.

---

21   Kevin Laval, Ibid

It is noteworthy that in late May, the security force at Fort Chaffee consisted of only four deputy marshals and five officers of the U.S. Park Police. The Park Police had been deputized as deputy marshals. They worked together with the military police but the MPs had no arrest authority over civilians. They could detain and escort only. The Marshals Service was the primary agency with arrest authority. This was ominous for future events.[22]

One refugee and his family, approved for release, spoke with a reporter in a story with no byline. He had been a policeman in the Batista government. He was imprisoned for fifteen years. He said that there were five-thousand criminals among the twenty-thousand persons populating Fort Chaffee. For their own protection the refugees elected barracks chiefs and posted guards. Meal tickets and IDs were the most stolen items.

The Southwest Times Record noted in a story with no by-line on May 23, that the post stockade had been opened to house Cuban refugees caught outside the fenced barracks area. These would now be the last of the refugees to be processed out of Chaffee. Many of those being held in the county jail were transferred to the stockade including three individuals accused of stealing a truck outside the base and two who were arrested in a Barling restaurant while visiting with an uncle of one of the men. The uncle was a volunteer on base. They just happened to sit down next to an INS agent that had interviewed one of them the week before. Oops![23]

Frustration and dissatisfaction built among the Cubans and their families. This brought on tighter security with more razor wire fences and new entry procedures. The base was placed on closed status. People had been coming onto the base to locate family members. An unidentified occupant of a passing car threw something

22 *Southwest Times Record*, vol. 86 # 142, May 21, 1980
23 Joanne Norton, Ibid

over the fence. This resulted in everyone being subject to search.

Adding to the frustration on the part of the refugees and their families was the fact that all refugee releases after the screening process was completed, had to then be approved in Washington DC. This was before computers and emails. In order to speed the process, all approvals were now handled in-house at Chaffee.

The new procedure involved screening by the INS. The refugee was then matched with family or sponsor. Additionally, if a family showed up and the refugee had been screened and found to have no health problems, they were free to take him and leave. A big problem in moving the refugees from Fort Chaffee was lack of adequate air service at Fort Smith. This new procedure was too little too late for some of the detainees.[24]

On May 24, Sebastian County deputies arrested two refugees two miles from Jenny Lind. This was in regard to a burglary. One of the refugees had to be treated at the hospital for hyperventilation following a foot chase. The two were identified as Parrado Hernandez Santos, thirty-three, and Viero Perez Lazzaro, twenty-four. There had been several calls to the sheriff's office concerning these two.

The break-in was at the home of Addy McCray. There the burglars made coffee and cooked some meat. They later showed up at the home of Earl Dodd near Greenwood—and he fired a warning shot with his shotgun. Ms. McCray said she wasn't afraid of them. "I would have fed them if they asked. They may carry me off but they're not going to run me off," she said.[25]

There was a problem determining who had jurisdiction over these Cubans. Sheriff Bill Cauthron, concerned about security, held a meeting about jurisdiction. They

24 *Southwest Times Record,* vol.86 # 144, May 23, 1980
25 Richard Break, *Southwest Times Record*, vol. 86 # 145, May 24, 1980

REFUGEE BOXING MATCH AT CHAFFEE

determined that the sheriff's deputies and state police have the right to stop anyone they suspect of being off base illegally and check their papers. The military police could act on base but only to protect persons and property. The U.S. Marshals and Park Police had jurisdiction both on and off base. This would cause a lot of problems in the near future.[26]

The Ku Klux Klan had a solution to the problem. The Grand Wizard of the KKK, the infamous David Duke, showed up in Fort Smith. He held a press conference in Creekmore Park. Only some media types and a few Frisbee players were in attendance:

26   Richard Break, *Southwest Times Record*, vol. 86 # 146, May 25, 1980

Stop the influx of Cuban refugees into this country! Train those who are willing to go back to Cuba and fight to overthrow Castro!

Duke went on to explain that the training should take place outside the U.S. on some island. He sat on a picnic table surrounded by fifteen white-robed klansmen. Close by a volleyball game went on undisturbed.

We think that Cuba should be freed from Castro but don't think it is a good idea to have a massive influx of Cuban refugees.

He went on to explain that the KKK is an anticommunist organization and that there are about one-hundred and fifty ready to go to Cuba and overthrow the Castro regime. He only wanted the U.S. government involved in this to support volunteers. He expressed the opinion that any Cubans living here who refused to be a part of the invasion should be deported to another Spanish speaking country.

We have no great dislike for Cubans, but we don't want them coming to the U.S. I can't see giving them free medical care and putting them on welfare; and then their children on welfare and then their children's children on welfare...the Klan is the only organization willing to speak up on this.

PAUL BROWN WORKING ON REFUGEE RECORDS IN THE GUARD SHACK

Earlier in the day, there had been a parade in front of Fort Chaffee consisting of around twenty-four persons sporting "White Power" shirts and holding anti-Cuban posters. Some passersby cheered and some cursed. A later rally for the Klan at Creekmore Park drew about one-hundred-fifty people. Duke spoke for forty-five minutes. His speech was full of racism. "Their country for them and our country for us!" he shouted and this

drew loud applause from his minions.[27] This was all being mixed in a cauldron that was about to boil over.

On the evening of May 26, an announcement boomed
over the public address system at the opening night of
the Old Fort Days Rodeo in Fort Smith. All off duty
sheriff's deputies were to report to the courthouse.
There had been an uprising of about one hundred Cubans at Fort Chaffee and about forty made it off the
post. Riot gear equipped police responded to the call.
The escapees made it to the Rye Hill area and were
rounded up by the Arkansas State Police with no incident. Those recaptured filled four army buses, patrol
cars and private vehicles. There were many more than
the forty reported.[28]

CHAFFEE GUARD SHACK

The root cause of the unrest was the slow processing
of the refugees for eventual release to sponsors and families. There was a lot of anger. The problem was being
made worse by the presence on base of many families
seeking their relatives among the detainees. One of the
refugees, Pedro Monteagudo, a medical doctor, said that
there were communist agitators among the population

27 Ray Robinson, Ibid
28 Kevin Laval, *Southwest Times Record*, vol. 86 # 149, May 28, 1980

also. He said these agitators provoked two hundred and twenty-five refugees by telling them that their release was being delayed to enable local businessmen to make more money and that the Ku Klux Klan was threatening them. The agitators told them also their relatives, who came to retrieve them, were being beaten by military personnel.[29]

The unrest was likewise causing a fear in the surrounding communities and among elected officials including the governor, Bill Clinton, who was on scene. In response to the unrest, he activated sixty-five members of the Arkansas National Guard and called in seventeen units of the Arkansas State Police to assist in perimeter security. The federal coordinator meanwhile insisted that the situation was well in control. One official described the disturbance as "little more than a college panty raid."

Sheriff Bill Cauthron called the panty raid comment, "The biggest understatement since Noah said he thought it was going to rain."[30]

Clinton insisted that the security was totally inadequate when General Drummond told him that Gate 9 near Jenny Lind was open and unguarded. Gate 9 was where many of the refugees left the base. Tension between local and state officials and the Federal officials who were in charge of the operation increased. Even though Fort Smith police controlled traffic on Highway 22 in front of the main gate, for a while the military denied local law enforcement access to the post. Chief Deputy Marshal Jim Smith said he had not asked for the help of any local officials. Fort Smith Chief of Police Henry Oliver responded that he was responsible for the safety of the people of Fort Smith and that Sheriff Bill Cauthron was responsible for the safety of the people

29   Richard Break, *Southwest Times Record*, vol. 86 #146, May 25, 1980
30   *Southwest Times Record*, vol. 86 #146, May 25, 1980 (no byline)

of Sebastian County—and they felt they had no choice but to react.

City administrator Steve Lease was even more direct. He called the federal officials irresponsible and incompetent. The truth came out, according to Lease, because local law enforcement found three hundred Cubans milling around outside the base and rounded them up. This roundup was going on at the same time as federal officials were saying nothing was going on.

It's a situation that has developed that never should have developed and we will exercise control to protect the best interests of the citizens of this area...the only accountability and responsibility evidenced in these circumstances has been from local officials, state police and the governor's office.

The purpose of the press conference was to broadside the erroneous information coming from Chaffee authorities.

We are concerned with what is happening outside the base. That is our responsibility....The city has no intention of doing anything in conflict with the state or federal programs, policies or best interest of the nation. At the same time, a lot of the situation could have been avoided with adequate pre-conferencing with local officials, with adequate planning in terms of security and with a lot more coordination and active communication.[31]

This latest breakout followed an earlier incident when two hundred Cubans broke through a sawhorse and rope barricade and ran down Main Street shouting slogans such as "Cuba Libre." The Cuban leaders repaired the barricades and quieted the crowd. General

---

31 *Southwest Times Record*, vol. 90 # 148, May 27, 1980 (no byline)

Drummond praised the group leaders for their actions. "We didn't draw a weapon or use a club."

This earlier incident, of course, did little to calm the present fears and concerns outside the post. Governor Clinton called President Carter and talked candidly with him. The President promised to get back with him within twenty-four hours. Meanwhile Adj. General Jimmy "Red" Jones of the Arkansas National Guard said that his soldiers would cover all seven gates into the facility.[32]

On May 28, Editor Jack Moseley summed up the attitude of the community in an editorial. It is quoted in its entirety.

For the safety of the people of this community and the Cuban refugees, another mass escape must not happen.

It was a miracle that the Monday night escape of some 200 refugees through and unguarded gate of the military post did not result in a violent incident with horrible consequences. The potential for bloodshed, misunderstanding and eruptions of irrational behavior was horrendous.

Two hours after the escape, a SWTR photographer was taking pictures of refugees being herded along Old Jenny Lind Road, while a Chaffee spokesman was assuring this office that "no one got off post." Tuesday, officials at the fort said there was a breakdown in communications.

That's not all that broke down. There was a breakdown in security when several hundred people participated in a mass demonstration that federal authorities compared to a college "panty raid,"

32   Kevin Laval, *Southwest Times Record*, vol. 90 #150, May 29, 1980

then immediately ran out into the populated civilian countryside without anyone attempting to stop them.

Federal authorities, who have insisted they have the refugee situation well under control, Monday night said they did not ask for state and local assistance to return some 200 Cubans to the military post. Thank God state police, sheriff's deputies and city police rounded up the refugees before something tragic occurred, whether the civilian lawmen's help was requested or not.

If the straight facts are given the people of this area are largely tolerant and understanding. They are neither violent or vicious. But like people everywhere, they have natural fears that are aroused by misinformation, rumors and any indication they are not being given the whole truth.

Likewise, the refugees must be made to understand exactly what is happening to them and why they must remain at Fort Chaffee until their backgrounds are checked and they are properly processed for release into American society.

We do not know what triggered the refugee actions Monday evening. Perhaps it was the heat, perhaps dissatisfaction caused by Cuban-American relatives who could not get refugees out of the main compound, perhaps fear of the Ku Klux Klan as some refugees stated. To assure that the refugees are not triggered again by fear, frustration or misinformation, we believe a Spanish speaking American soldier should be placed at every barracks building to keep the Cubans informed, answer their questions and listen for signs of unrest or trouble.

*Finally, somebody must be given clear responsi-
bility and authority to maintain order and security. That should come directly from the man in
the White House. We are sick of hearing that the
military police cannot arrest aliens on a military
post, that arrests can be made only by U. S. Marshals while only the FBI can investigate a crime,
that the department of Justice says one group has
authority while the superiors of that group will
not give the orders to use that authority.*

*The President of the United States made the deci-
sion to send the Cubans here; he has the responsibility to see the refugee relocation effort operates
without the mass confusion that has existed since
the first planeload of Cubans touched down here.*

*When authority is assigned clearly, those given
the responsibility must be supplied with the necessary manpower to carry out their job efficiently
and completely.*

*We commend Gov. Bill Clinton for coming here to
personally calm public fears and demand action
to insure the public safety from the highest level
of the federal government. The people of this
area have accepted the Cuban refugees, although
no one here asked that they be brought to Fort
Chaffee. The people are entitled to assurances
of security and straight information from no less
than the president of The United States.*

*This newspaper continues to have sympathy and
understanding for the genuine refugees who fled
Fidel Castro's communist dictatorship. Their
safety and ultimate freedom in our society also
is at stake. They should clearly understand the
consequences of any unthinking act. To date,
no American citizen here has been physically*

harmed. For the sake of the people of this area
and the refugees, let's keep it that way.[33]

More troops went to Chaffee and they were in the
Arkansas National Guard. Governor Bill Clinton in
a meeting at the Fort Smith Civic Center said he was
demanding that a perimeter be built inside the fort to
prevent additional escapes. At the same time, he pro-
posed the closure of the gate on the south side of the
base, Gate 9, from where most of the refugees had
fled—and add fifty to seventy-five security personnel
from the GSA and ten more deputy marshals. It was his
understanding that military police, now with law enforcement authority courtesy of an order from President
Carter, could detain any refugees trying to leave. He
was going to use the additional ANG troops to patrol
the outside of the base. "We will plug the holes," he
said.[34]

The fears and anger of the area residents were real
and potentially violent. Some living near Jenny Lind
had guns and had threatened the refugees. One person
reported that refugees threw rocks at her car as she
drove through them.

The letters to the editor of the *Southwest Times Record* also took a distinct anti-refugee tilt. Phillip V.
Brown wrote:

Why are we the trash can of the world? Castro
has rid his country of his misfits and some spies.
They are taking jobs Americans need. Ship em
back or send them to another country. Or make
sure they are gainfully employed and applying
for citizenship.[35]

Inside Fort Chaffee, things were not getting better.
Resentment on delays in processing was again reaching

33   Joanne Norton, *Southwest Times Record*, vol. 90 #149 , May 28, 1980
34   Becky Meeks, *Southwest Times Record*, vol. 90 # 151, May 30, 1980
35   Letters to the Editor, *Southwest Times Record*, vol. 90 # 153, June 1, 1980

critical mass. On Wednesday, May 28, a crowd of one thousand marched toward the main gate demanding release. Victor Valdez, a former political prisoner who had lived in the United States for four months was credited with calming this disturbance. On Friday, three hundred protesting Cubans blocked the main street and threatened a hunger strike. No one tried to escape and the military maintained a low profile. They crossed the sawhorse and rope barrier and chanted "Libertad." They carried their cots out and sat down on them. Military and federal officers blocked them from the main gate area. Several mess hall workers couldn't home on time as they had to leave by the back gate. Mr. Valdez once again calmed the crowd around 3:30 p.m. in the afternoon by promising them that the U.S. authorities were going to address their demands. Ironically, the protests were adding to the problem of which they complained. Many times departures were delayed because the refugees scheduled to get on an outward bound bus couldn't be found because they were among those milling around in protest.[36]

With the resentment and anger on the inside of the compound boiling and the fear, resentment and anger on the outside reaching fever pitch as well and explosion was imminent. It came on Sunday.

36 Kevin Laval and David Edds, *Southwest Times Record*, vol. 90 #152, May 31, 1980

III

JUNE 1, 1980

SUNDAY, JUNE 1,1980, BEGAN as a normal day. Some refugees engaged in a quiet sit-in around the main gate. This was shattered when about three hundred Cubans bolted toward the gate and poured over the wall as military police stood by and watched. The Cubans headed west on Highway 22 before being stopped by Arkansas State Police about three quarters of a mile from the main gate. Swinging sticks and sometimes striking them, the Troopers herded them back to base. About one-hundred refugees gathered inside the gate and listened to one of them saying, "Carter bad, the police are bad, and we should set fire to the barracks."

The crowd dispersed. However, about 5 p.m., the demonstrators reappeared. *Southwest Times Record* reporter Kevin Laval was in the press building at the time and heard the approaching crowd shouting 'Libertad!" He had visited with a refugee taking part in the peaceful demonstration that morning and this came as a bit of a surprise. About thirty refugees rushed a Tulsa TV crew who sought shelter inside the press building protected by club-wielding MPs. Laval heard shots and four-hundred Cubans ran back into the compound. As they climbed the front wall again, the MPs stood aside and watched as they were forbidden to use force to stop them.

MAIN GATE AT FORT CHAFFEE

This was contrary to Governor Clinton's understanding based on assurances from the White House. The state troopers, now reinforced, began following the refugees west—not allowing them to cross to the north side of Highway 22. Rocks began flying—and for a while, the police were on the defensive. Several troopers took cover—but newly-arrived-sheriff's deputies along with the troopers charged, firing shots, some of which struck at least three of the refugees. The refugees began to fall back behind the fence, still throwing rocks. Laval and the others in the press building were advised to evacuate. They jumped from a back window ten feet to the ground and fled in a car.[1] Helicopters were overhead and the injured were taken to the field hospital.

Meanwhile outside the front gate, three state troopers collared one man and beat him with nightsticks. Plumes of smoke began to rise over the base. The barricades, guard shack and two mess halls were set on fire.

1   Kevin Laval and Ray Robinson, *Southwest Times Record,* vol. 90 # 154, June 2, 1980

During the melee, club-wielding-Cuban vigilantes sporting white armbands came to the aid of the police. The various factions of Cubans began fighting among themselves. By late Sunday evening, an uneasy calm settled over the base and members of the white-armband group stood by every corner of the housing area. Some posed with reporters for pictures and offered protection. Others swept the area with brooms, cleaning away the debris from the guard shack that had been burned. Others guarded firemen and volunteers who were moping up operations at the various building fires. The firefighters credited these Cubans with helping save the buildings. Of the "white-armband police" Deputy Marshal Jim Smith said, "They helped us kick ass." By about 10 o'clock that evening, it was all over. Kevin Laval stated in his article:

I left the post at 10:30 p.m. driving through broken glass, smoked filled air and damaged automobiles, where only hours before I had enjoyed a friendly conversation with a friendly refugee.

"It was like a war out there," cried a woman waiting to be treated in the St. Edward ER. The hospital called in extra Personnel. Soldiers guarded the doors and helped unload injured people. Fifteen patients, said to be critical—including three Cubans, were the first to be treated with gunshot wounds. There was another with critical knife wounds.

One of the shooting victims had wounds in his chest and abdomen while another bullets in his chest and both legs. The remaining gunshot victim—hit in the head and arm—had a possible skull fracture. A state trooper was treated for cuts from flying glass and rocks. A Cuban man had a heart attack.[2]

2   Joanne Norton, *Southwest Times Record*, vol. 90 # 154, June 2, 1980

JIM SPEARS

CUBAN REFUGEES LIVING IN FORT CHAFFEE BARRACKS

Things were also not calm amongst the native Barlingites. What started as a group of good-natured sightseers turned into a near mob. Earlier, they watched a group of six Cubans leave the base—picking wild flowers in an open field without comment. The Barlingites laughed as they watched U.S. Marshals chase the seemingly playful Cubans back into the restricted area of the post. As it grew darker, they saw smoke rising from the base. After watching police car after police car pass, they became angry.

Nearly the entire community of Barling, Arkansas, population three thousand, gathered on Highway 22. They were frightened and business at *Jerry Barling's Gun City* was brisk. They moved toward Fort Chaffee but were stopped at Lock and Dam 13 road by riot-gear-clad police. Some people had signs and some had bats. They were all angry and fearful. One person waved an American flag. Many yelled curses at the MPs blocking the road. Five men and one woman were taken into custody when they refused to disperse when ordered to do so by police.[3]

Captain Deloin Causey of the Arkansas State Police was called in to calm them. He told them in answer to shouted questions, "We may have shot one—and one Cuban has been found dead, killed by another refugee."

One man yelled, "One? Just one? We need a hundred!"

The crowd went wild, cursing the military police nearby. After again quieting down, someone asked about the possibility of some getting out.

Causey told them, "They'll not cross our line. We have shotguns and will use deadly force if necessary."

The crowd roared approval. "I want to kill one of those sobs!" one person yelled.

---

3   Mike Crowden, *Southwest Times Record*, vol. 90 # 154, June 2, 1980

"Let em starve to death," said another.

Asked by one if he had the right to bear arms Causey said, "Yes, on your own property."

"This is our property!" yelled another sending the crowd into a frenzy.

Finally, Causey calmed them down and it became like a town picnic with teenagers holding hands and young people pushing baby strollers. Men stood around talking about President Carter's shortcomings. Then a guy on a motorcycle sped up to the police line, raced his engine and then burst through the line. Police flailed at him with night sticks. This set the crowd off again:

We need a thousand more like that. These damned army people ain't going to do nothing. Why don't you go beat on those Cubans instead of us Americans.

One guy carrying two shotguns was escorted away from the area. After being assured that calm had been restored, many wandered back to their houses. Some milled around the side of the road while others told stories about what had happened and what should have been done to prevent it.

"Well, at least we got one of 'em," a lady said as she walked back to her house.[4]

How and why did this type of thing happen again? Editor Jack Moseley had been with Governor Clinton in all his meetings with base officials since his arrival on site at 8:30 p.m. Sunday night during the riot. Army officials had not yet received "official" authority to use "necessary force." Civilian authorities blamed the lack of action on the part of the military for the breakouts the previous Tuesday, as well as the two that occurred on Sunday. This lack of authority came as a surprise to Gene Eidenberg, President Carter's representative

4   Kevin Laval, *Southwest Times Record*, vol. 90 # 155, June 3, 1980

on the scene, as he personally gave Governor Clinton assurance a week ago that the army had the authority to use force to maintain order and to keep the refugees contained.

The Department of Justice also assured the officials at the fort that it was legal for them to contain by "necessary force" the refugees on base. However, the army said until they received specific orders from a superior military command, they could not use force. After a more than hour and a half meeting between Clinton and General Drummond, the governor said there was no clear understanding of who was in charge. Clinton opined that the relocation operation seemed to run by committee. It was not until after 4 a.m. Monday, following a conference with his commanders, that Drummond received the official authority to use force. State officials, including Clinton, refused to blame Drummond who was following the only orders he received from his military commanders. It was a communication problem according to Clinton, but all was not peaches and cream between military and civilian authorities.[5]

General Drummond denied there was any breakdown in communications with the military higher ups. He was still not happy, but not complaining, about the physical response of the local authorities. He indicated that they used the force they deemed appropriate, leaving the impression he did not share that feeling. Senator Dale Bumpers was not pleased at all with General Drummond's response to the disturbance and referred to it as a terrible breakdown in communication. He called the whole operation a "comedy of errors.

The fact that the military commander didn't have the authority to restrain these people and keep them under control (on a military base) just blows my mind.

5   Kevin Laval, *Southwest Times Record*, vol. 90 # 156, June 4, 1980

IV

THE AFTERMATH

THE BASE WAS RELATIVELY quiet the next day. Children played near the barracks and the milling groups of detainees were not present. The forty-six individuals who instigated the riot were now in the stockade. Ironically, refugee processing which was the root cause of the riots in the first place, were suspended for a few days.

Delay was in the DNA of Governor Clinton. This was commonly referred to as "Clinton Time." He was scheduled to meet with the Fort Smith Board of Directors at 1:30 a.m. Monday, but was held up with General Drummond who was attempting to get authorization to use force. As 3 a.m. approached, Director Leonard Bogoslavsky quipped, "When this is all over, I'm going to ask the directors to chip in and buy the governor a watch."

The others agreed, but the sentiment was that since they had waited this long they couldn't leave now.[1]

Still helping to maintain order was the "white-armband police." Their weapons were clubs and crude knives made from available material. Patrolling in

---

1   Joanne Norton, *Southwest Times Record*, vol. 90 # 154, June 2, 1980

groups of twenty-fifty on every block, their stated purpose was to prevent any more incidents like Sunday:

*We'll line up and stop them. We will always fight
for peace at Fort Chaffee to show the Americans
we are entitled to all the privileges they offer.
Show America we are grateful. If we can we will
also go to Cuba to fight for freedom there.*

There was also an informal intelligence-gathering
network. The desire was to make sure rioting doesn't
happen again. Arturo—his last name was not used to
protect his family back in Cuba—said:

*Orders have been given by our leaders to get
whoever started it. There are about three to four
hundred troublemakers. We knew it (the riot) was
going to happen before it did. Those people are
now in hiding. They are moving through different
crowds now where they can go unnoticed. There
were about four or five brains behind this thing
yesterday. They are the same ones as in the other
incidents. Then they get the backing of the stupid
weak-minded numbers.*

In fluent English, Arturo indicated that the leaders
had a meeting and directed the refugees to take down the
names of the troublemakers. "If the few (rioters) keep
fooling around, they will just kill them." He explained
that the Cubans didn't fear the Americans outside the
gate—with the possible exception of the KKK from the
stories they had heard. It was just a process of getting
to know each other. Other Cubans expressed their grat-
itude and feeling of duty to the Americans. Arturo even
defended some of the rioters. It was mainly frustration.
They weren't Castro's agents but just played his games.[2]

Steve Beck, a recreational coordinator on base, also
defended the refugees. The actions of a few gave a bad

2   Richard Break, *Southwest Times Record,* vol. 90 # 154 June 2, 1980

name to the larger group."We are just sick of not hearing about the sincere, dedicated refugees which are the
majority of the people we have here." He was furious
with what had been broadcast during the riot. "These
people are not criminals in our sense of the word." He
showed two guys clutching baseball bats and sleeping.
"When I left last night I had to leave my car. These
two guys put on baseball helmets and marched around
guarding it all night. They would have given their lives
just to protect my car. Any of them would give their
lives to protect me. One of the nearby refugees told the
reporter: "We are against anything that can make Castro
laugh at the United States."[3]

Changes were coming. Washington sent word that
this type of thing was not to happen again. By Friday
Governor Clinton and the local law enforcement officials felt better about the security arrangements. The
U.S. Marshals and their intelligence network within the
population started an investigation. The marshals reported to INS. Concertina wire completely surrounded
the enclosure making large movements of individuals
extremely difficult.

A surprise raid confiscated all weapons, drugs and
other contraband. This included the weapons carried by
the "white armband police" who had been so helpful to
the authorities during the riot. There were seven hundred and thirty-six can openers, home-made knives and
other makeshift weapons found in a three-hour search.
Initiated by the request of the refugees, it seemed more
than likely that the self-appointed-police force was not
entirely benevolent.

Twenty Park Police and sixty-two Military Police
conducted the search. While Military personnel standing elbow to elbow cordoned off the area, civilian

---

3   Becky Meeks, *Southwest Times Record*, vol. 90 # 156, June 7, 1980

authorities told the Cubans to drop whatever weapons they had. They complied with no incident.

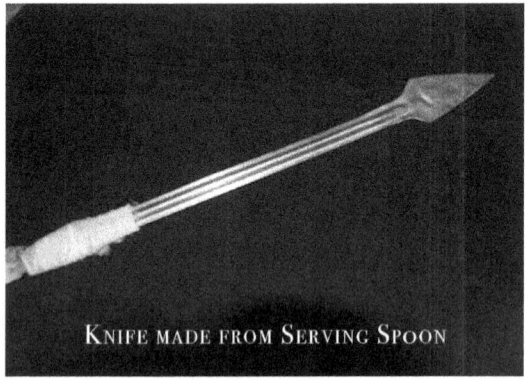

KNIFE MADE FROM SERVING SPOON

The round-up netted the following: one hundred and nine aluminum-army-cot ties, thirty wooden-army-cot ties, twenty-five bunk-bed spacers, one hundred assorted knives, five hundred can openers, one homemade tomahawk, four baseball bats, two homemade torches, numerous stones and pieces of broken glass, several empty rifle shells and one ten-pound ham.

No guns were found despite persistent reports. The knives included some from the mess hall, but most were made from aluminum-window-screen moldings that had been bent and ground to a point on one end. The can openers were part of a kit the refugees received when they arrived. The torches were rags tied to sticks. The empty shells were old and probably dug up from underneath the barracks. Most interesting was the tomahawk—a stone around which window-screen molding had been wrapped. Telephone wire secured the rock, about the size of two fists, to a foot-long-aluminum handle.

Not all contraband were weapons. Authorities seized fourteen bottles of homemade brew in various stages of processing. The officers also took their stills. This answered one question. "Now we know where all the apples and sugar went!" Several days prior, mess hall burglars stole large amounts of sugar.

In addition, the authorities found several bottles of prescription drugs and a stolen passport.[4]

The circumstances required that the attitude of the whole operation change. General Drummond said more problems would occur but they would be inside the compound. The refugees were frustrated to be housed behind barbed wire.

"The anger level is pretty high, the frustration level is pretty high—and the anxiety level is pretty high," said Drummond. He was unsure how long it would take to move all the refugees out to sponsors. There was a hard-core group that would be difficult to place.

The Cuban personality was a factor to consider in running the base.

Everyone is a leader or a spokesman for the group. There must be communication and it requires firm fixed procedures. If exceptions are made for some, the others will demand like treatment.

Turning over refugees to family members on the base was an example of an eliminated exception to the general rule. On one occasion, troops had to be deployed to stop some families from coming onto the base to get their relatives. The procedure was for all refugees, when released, to be sent to the Fort Smith airport with a ticket. The families could then pick them up there—and the government got a refund on the ticket if it wasn't used. Drummond continued:

This whole business is new to us. We are not in the army to tend to Cubans...we're here to string wire and fire cannons. Tending to Cubans was FEMA's job. The military was to act as the

4   Kevin Laval, *Southwest Times Record*, vol. 90 # 156, June 7, 1980

hotel owners. The military has taken a beating on public criticism because troops didn't stop refugees who rushed the main gate. The Army's lack of action goes back to a 19th century prohibition passed by congress that prohibits the use of military troops against civilians.[5]

At the time of the riot, the Justice Department was in charge of security. There were a total of seven U.S. deputy marshals for over nineteen-thousand Cubans. Following an executive order from the White House, changes were made. The number of military police expanded from fifty to one thousand. Triple strands of concertina wire placed around the entire enclave, stopped large numbers of people from moving in and out. Armed reaction troops stood on standby.

The gates were guarded. The U.S. Marshals Service was no longer responsible for fort-wide security. Moonlighting-off-duty-local police ran the stockade under the supervision of the marshals. There were sixty Park Police on duty—and twenty-four, three-man patrols acted as beat cops going after any illegal activity inside the compound.

The relocation efforts, up to that time, put more than $11.8 million dollars into the local economy—mostly through salaries, food and services. GSA contracts for vehicle rentals, motel stays and equipment rounded out the field. Medical expenses alone accounted for $144,000 of the total.[6]

5   Becky Meeks, Ibid
6   Kevin Laval, Ibid

V

LAW ENFORCEMENT AND THE COURT

NOW THAT THERE WAS a police force inside the compound and an operating jail, there needed to be a court to adjudicate and hand out punishment. That led to La Corte del Magistrado, the Court of the Magistrate. The United States Magistrate is the inferior court to the United States District Court. The district judge is a presidential appointment for life. The magistrate is hired by the district court for a term of years.

In criminal matters, this court hears misdemeanor cases, arraignments, pre-trial matters or anything that the district court may assign including some matters before a jury.[1] That means that any misdemeanor criminal matter arising at Fort Chaffee, since it occurred on a federal military base, would fall under the jurisdiction of the magistrate court. That, of course, meant anything involving the Cubans that were on the base.

The United States Magistrate for the Western District of Arkansas in Fort Smith was Ned A. Stewart Jr. He became U.S. Magistrate in 1979. He was the first full-time magistrate for the western district. Before this, he was the United States commissioner in Texarkana. A

---

1   28 U.S. Code sec.636

part-time position, it's only duty was to arraign persons charged with a crime.

Paul X. Williams was the United States district judge for the Western District. Ned was a law clerk for Judge J. Smith Henley, a judge for the Eastern District. He also served as an assistant U.S. attorney from 1965-68. When a part time magistrate position opened up in Texarkana, Ned received the appointment. When a full-time position was established in Fort Smith, Judge Williams appointed him to an eight-year term.

The first Cubans to come before Ned in June referred to him as "Commandante" as that was the frame of authority for them. This seemed, to them at least, appropriate since they were on a military base surrounded by soldiers. When the Cubans arrived at Chaffee, there was no idea of the federal judiciary being involved. After the breakouts and the riot, it became obvious that there needed to be a judicial presence as the military couldn't be used to enforce criminal civilian law. This was the old Posse Commitatus left over from the Reconstruction era referred to by General Drummond. President Carter ordered the military to take care of it and the military contacted the Department of Justice. They determined that federal-law enforcement should be brought in. They asked Magistrate Stewart—and he agreed to do it.

At that time, there were very few people in the western Arkansas/eastern Oklahoma area who spoke Spanish. There was no system of certified court interpreters and the refugee population spoke no English. This was a problem and it needed to be addressed. Stewart did know a lawyer's wife who had lived in Cuba and taught Spanish at the local community college. Her name was Rachael Smith. He contacted Rachael and she agreed to help as the court's interpreter.[2]

2 Interview with Ned Stewart, April 8, 2017

Rachael recalls returning from a trip to Canada and receiving a call from Magistate Stewart. "It was in the airport and I must have been paged as it was long before the cell phone." Magistrate Stewart explained the problem and Mrs. Smith agreed to help. "I had knowledge of Cuba as I lived there my first three years of college." Her father, Colonel Ernest Vance Cameron was a military attaché to Cuba under the Military Assistance Defense Pact. He was an advisor to the Cuban government of Fulgencio Batista. This was in the middle 1950s.

Rachael remained in the United States to finish high school but went to college in Cuba. She was the only American in the school—Univseridad Santo Tomas de Villanueva. She knew no Spanish when she moved there but picked it up easily. In August of 1958, her parents decided it was getting too dangerous for her to remain there. There were a lot of student uprisings and insurgencies. Considering her father's position, she was a likely target for kidnapping. She transferred to the University of Oklahoma as her father had some contacts there. She decided to major in languages as she was already fluent in Spanish. "I loved the Cuban people and the language but I had no formal background in Spanish and had to start in the beginning class. The regular students hated me. The Cubans had a distinct dialect like someone from Brooklyn would have. It was a lazy Spanish that I had to overcome."

She recalls that they first set up a traveling court inside the compound at Fort Chaffee. The traveling team consisted of her, Magistrate Stewart, his secretary Janie Gazzola, Assistant U.S. Attorney Neal Kirkpatrick and P.K. Holmes as the appointed counsel for the Cubans charged with offenses. The building used at that time may have been an old chapel.[3]

---

3   Interview with Rachel Smith, February 8, 2010

P.K. Holmes, now the U.S. District Judge for the Western District of Arkansas, was a young associate at the law firm of Warner and Smith in Fort Smith. He had been with the firm since 1978 when he graduated law school. He recalls that almost immediately as the Cubans arrived at Fort Chaffee in May, criminal situations began to occur within the population. Judge Paul X. Williams appointed him on some criminal matters in the court and he requested that the young lawyer take these cases involving the Cubans too. "After consultation with the firm, it was agreed that I would do so as it would be great experience for a young lawyer. I received small compensation on a case by case basis."[4] It was $20 per hour out-of-court time and $30 per hour for in court.[5]

He recalls that with the first cases, prisoners were transported from the compound to downtown Fort Smith. This proved to be impractical for the misdemeanors, so Magistrate Stewart decided to relocate inside Fort Chaffee. He worked out the details. Holmes considered Rachael Smith as part of his staff, but, in fact, she was the only interpreter available to the court. The two of them would go into the compound to interview witnesses. There were mainly misdemeanors and a few felonies. The felonies were tried before the district judge with a jury and always in the federal courthouse downtown.

One felony case recalled was that of Raul Matos. He had been accused of a vicious assault on another detainee. He was in a wheelchair as a result of an injury in Cuba.

At first he did not trust me or Rachael and did not communicate. Slowly he came around to trust us and his case was a three-day jury trial. The jury deliberated for sometime and found him guilty. He had been held in the stockade at Chaffee all

4   Interview with P. K. Holmes, March 22, 2010
5   Interview with P. K. Holmes, March 22, 2010

during the time that the charges were pending. Judge Williams just sentenced him to time served. The victim had been hurt pretty bad. I later had a chance to talk to Harper Jackson who had been on the jury. He said it was hard to convict him as several on the jury had been in bar fights during their lives and to them the incident was not that big of a deal.

It is interesting as this writers experience later indicated that more leniency was shown the Cubans by the juries than one would expect.

Another case involved a forgery allegation. Judge Tom Eisele of the eastern district of Arkansas had come from Little Rock to help with the increased caseload. The assistant U.S. attorney assigned to the Cuban cases was Neal Kirkpatrick, "Neal was known for having a pretty hot temper at times," Holmes said.

A negotiated plea of guilty had been reached and the witnesses were allowed to go to their sponsors around the country to start a new life. When the defendant appeared before the judge and questions were asked of him concerning the elements of the crime he answered no to several of them and Judge Eisele refused to accept the plea. Since the witnesses were gone the government had to dismiss the charges. Neal was angry. It was an issue of language and understanding and not a conspiracy to defeat the government's case but it mattered not to Neal.[6]

The workload got too heavy and P.K. had to give it up even though my office partner Gene Wahl had been taking some of the cases to help out.

6   Holmes interview, ibid

VI

ABAGADO DEFENSOR PUBLICO

A FRONT-PAGE ARTICLE IN on October 1, 1980, ad-
dressed the possibility of establishing a branch of the
Federal Public Defender's office in Fort Smith. The 8th
U.S. Circuit Court of Appeals examined the proposal.
Approved by judges in the western districts of Arkansas
and Missouri for the Federal Public Defender's office in
Kansas City, it dealt with the overload of cases result-
ing from the Cuban refugee situation.

COURT OF THE MAGISTRATE (LAS CORTE DEL MAGISTRADO)
ON THE BENCH (CENTER) JUDGE NED STEWART; ON THE
LEFT, JANIE GAZOLLA, U.S. MARSHALL; AT TABLE, (L-R) LEO
MARTINEZ, LUIS BELTHAU, & JIM SPEARS; U.S. MARSHALLS
IN FOREGROUND

In making the proposal, Magistrate Stewart estimated that the cases were up to about three hundred a
month. When he held Friday court on the base, sometimes as many as seventy-five were on his docket. Most
of the crimes were misdemeanors. The refugees couldn't
pay fines because they had no money. Therefore, jail
time was imposed as punishment. That fact entitled the
defendants to a court-appointed attorney under federal
law. The branch office would only open as long as needed. The original plan called for the office to be open
five months. It operated for seventeen. The staff would
be the attorney, a secretary and an interpreter.[1]

*These would be full-time employees. It ended
up with two interpreters/investigators and my
secretary was converted to a federal employee
along with an office allowance to defray my rent
and utilities.*

At the time, as previously mentioned, appointed attorneys received $20 per hour for out-of-court time and
$30 per hour for in-court time. For logistical reasons,
Magistrate Stewart appointed only one volunteer attorney, P.K. Holmes, to handle all the Cuban cases. When
Holmes could handle no more, Gene Wahl stepped in.
Stewart believed that a full-time lawyer and staff was
cheaper in the long run. In the story, Holmes explained
why it took twice as long to prepare a defense for a refugee than for an English-speaking defendant:

*Everything you say has to be interpreted for him
and everything he says has to be interpreted for
you. They don't understand our legal system because they don't have much of one at all. They
understand the words but they don't always understand the concepts....Some of them say they*

---

1   Ray Robinson, *Southwest Times Record*, vol. 87 # 275, October 1, 1980

don't want lawyers because they don't know what lawyers are for.[2]

This is the place in the narrative that the author becomes a part of the story. I graduated from law school in 1973, and went to work as an associate in the Sam Sexton Law Firm. Having political ambitions, I ran unsuccessfully for prosecuting attorney in 1978. Shortly thereafter, I decided to open my own law office. I was toiling in the trenches of private practice when my office mate, Gene Wahl, told me about the possibility of a public defender's job. This was before the article ran in the paper. He wasn't interested but I found it intriguing and put in my application.

The interview took place on the 2nd floor of the Federal post office and courthouse on the west side of South 6th Street. During my interview, I recall only one question and answer. *Why did I want to give up my law practice to take this temporary job?* I answered that I wanted to be a part of history and show the world that our system of justice is fair and impartial. I meant it. Evidently this made an impression and they hired me. The idea of a steady government paycheck was appealing along with the hope it could develop into something more permanent.

I had never worked for the government before and my introduction to the bureaucracy was interesting. Immediately after my hiring, a fine gentleman named Phil Moomaw, who worked out of the Springfield, MO office, mentored me. He gave me a crash course in Federal Criminal Procedure—and the office practices expected.

One interesting requirement was to keep a log of everything I did. This was from the time I got to work until I went home. For example:

2   Ned Stewart interview, ibid

Phone call from Janie Gazzola, magistrate secretary informing of tomorrow's docket, or conference with Gus Saucedo my investigator.

I kept these notes in a binder and each week I mailed a copy to Kansas City.

In addition to Phil, I was blessed with visits from Norman Lynch. He was the epitome of a Washington bureaucrat, tightly wound with a skinny suit and narrow tie, all black. His title was Chief, Criminal Justice Act Division, Administrative Office of the U.S. Courts. Early in the process, after I hired my wife Dixie, I invited Norman—along with Phil Moomaw and possibly Ray Conrad, the Federal Public Defender in Kansas City—to the house for dinner. Everything went smoothly with a fine meal, drinks and lively conversation.

After dinner we sat in the living room talking about family and the job. Suddenly, I heard a scream from the stairway—and our three-year-old son John, stark naked, ran down the stairs and through the dining room in front of Phil, Ray and Norman. I was shocked. Then his horrified mother followed in hot pursuit. Everyone laughed. Son John, now under control and fast on his way back to his bed upstairs, squealed with delight. I wondered if they were going to change their minds about hiring me. They didn't. And the three-year-old streaker? He is now a foreign service officer at the U.S. Embassy in Mexico City working with USAID.

The next day, Mr. Lynch and I went on a tour of the compound—and to the courthouse to meet with Magistrate Stewart and U.S. District Judge Paul X. Williams. As a part of this expedition, we visited a female detainee housed in the Sebastian County jail.(There was no provision for females at the fort stockade.) Designed to hold a little more than eighty prisoners, the jail at that time was the top two floors of the county courthouse built in 1937. The sheriff got a per-prisoner dole to feed them. The Feds, then as now, also paid a daily charge to hold Federal prisoners. After interviewing the lady through an interpreter, I asked if there was anything I could do for her. She replied that she didn't like the food and that she wanted Cuban food. I told her that I could do nothing for her and that she would just have to eat what they gave her because she was in America now. This did not sit well with Mr. Lynch, whom I privately referred to as "The Suit." He dressed me down later in no uncertain terms. I was not culturally sensitive enough and much too "snarky" when I told her she would just have to eat what she was served. I thought he was going to fire me.

My staff, as mentioned earlier, was my secretary, Linda Hays and two Spanish speaking interpreter/investigators. Gustavo Saucedo was the first hired. Gus was from Eagle Pass, Texas. He and his mother ran a Mexican restaurant in Eagle Pass. Gus and his wife moved to the Fort Smith area when the call went out for Spanish speakers to work for the government during the relocation process.

No sooner had Gus gone to work for me than it looked like I was going to lose him. He was barred from the base! He had been seen, according to the MPs, giving marijuana to some of the juvenile detainees. This Gus denied vehemently. I believed him and went to bat on his behalf.

Military officers had intimidated me since my brief experience at Fort Knox, Kentucky in 1966, at ROTC basic camp. I had to go to the post headquarters and beg for Gus. I needed this guy. Sweating a little and with knocking knees, I approached the provost and successfully pleaded my first case as Federal public defender. From that point on, Gus did anything I asked of him.

Luis Beltran was my other interpreter/investigator. From Puerto Rico, as were many of the temporary workers here for the relocation, Luis was a large man with an afro hairdo. Gus was small with dark hair who looked like he stepped out of an ad for Brylcream.

We all worked well together. I sent them into the compound where they related to the Cubans much better than me. When they found the witnesses, I went with them to do formal interviews. About the only Spanish words I knew when this started was "adios" and "taco." It got to the point, however, that during an interview when one of the interpreters turned to me and began, "he said...," I interrupted to tell them that I knew what was going on. While I never learned to speak much Spanish, I understood much of those interrogations.

On a typical day in court, refugees, there for their initial appearance, sat in the anteroom with their hands cuffed. The judge's staff that traveled with him to Chaffee consisted of his secretary, Janie Gazzola and the court interpreter Rachael Smith. When everyone was in place, each defendant was called before the court. The judge asked him to rise and repeat his name and age— and then be seated. Judge Stewart advised the person of the charges pending and of the possible sentence. They were also told of their right to an attorney at government expense. (Obviously they had no money to hire one.) They were also advised of their right to a trial by jury in district court—and told that they could waive that and be tried by the current court. Each detainee was then called to the witness stand and sworn in, asked if they understood their rights—and if they wished to waive in writing their right to a jury trial. Judge Stewart made sure defendants understood, as best they could, the American system.

One defendant decided to not accept the court-appointed attorney. This made the newspaper with the headline "Cuban 'Perry Mason' loses case." On March 13, 1981, Jenny Deam reported that Alberto William Denza refused to accept a lawyer. He felt that having counsel was an admission of guilt. Judge Stewart made numerous attempts to convince him that he needed counsel—to no avail. Although he was found guilty of assaulting a Federal Protective Service agent, the man did a fairly credible job. He claimed he did not strike the female officer but merely raised his foot as if to kick her. He claimed the officer called him a "black monkey" and made profane references to his mother. "I am incapable of raising my hand against a woman...the words she used would have caused death or killing in Cuba," he claimed. He slammed his notes down on the table when he had concluded and declared, "I rest my case!" The agent denied all of his allegations. The judge and the interpreter, Rachael Smith theorized that he may have learned some of his tactics watching a show in Spanish at the base called "The Great Court" that pokes fun at lawyers.[3]

JUDGE NED STEWART, JR AND JIM SPEARS

Following my appointment to represent a defendant, we conducted a thorough interview before they were transported back to the stockade. Either Gus or Luis and I took them into the interview room. Some chattered

3   Jenny Deam, Southwest Times Record, vol. 91 #72, March 13, 1981

away before we could lay some ground rules. I ordered them, *"silencio!"* Then I asked them *"sientate por favor,"* followed by *"yo soy abagado defensor publico.'* Then, I asked them *"eres tu culpable or no culpable?"*

This all amounted to "shut up, sit down," "I'm your public defender," and "are you guilty or not guilty?" I learned how to ask their names and ages. This is how my relationship with my clients started and my ability with spoken Spanish ended. After the interview, the case was called back before the judge and a plea entered. My recollection is that many had to be tried. Cubans don't admit guilt readily and they knew that a finding of guilty or an admission wouldn't go well with them. They also mistrusted anyone from the government. Their experience in Cuba was certainly the basis for this. There were usually about thirty defendants on a docket in the early days, dwindling to two in December 1981—a month or two before the camp closed.

Following lunch, the judge heard cases from the previous week that were ready for trial or change of plea. The procedure for taking a guilty plea was similar to waiving the right to trial by jury. The court questioned the defendant extensively to insure that he knew his rights in the matter and that the plea was voluntary. In the trials, as in interviews, it took twice as long as usual since everything had to be interpreted. It was difficult to learn to work with an interpreter. I waited on the translation from English to Spanish and then the answer from Spanish to English, each time, every time, before asking another question. Communication was difficult. Translation was difficult. Colloquialisms in Spanish— as in English—vary from nation to nation and region to region. It was not unusual for Luis or Gus to nudge me during trial and say, "That's not what he said." We would then have a bench conference with the two lawyers and the interpreters to come to some understanding of the testimony.

After the entry of a guilty plea or a finding of guilty by the court, the probation officer prepared a pre-sentence report. He looked into the history of the defendant and interviewed him. In these cases, the only history known to the officials was that determined at the initial screening at Chaffee or wherever the refugee had been initially placed. Once this was done, he submitted a report to the court with copies to the U.S. Attorney and me. Based on this information, Magistrate Stewart rendered a sentence. This, of course was in an open hearing at our Chaffee courtroom.

Preparing these cases for trial was an adventure. Witnesses had to be located and interviewed. Sometimes we knew the witnesses as their names appeared on the charging sheets. Sometimes it was necessary for us to go into the compound to seek out persons identified by our clients. Security was strict following the break out in June.

SECURITY BADGE AND TEE SHIRT

Each person authorized to enter the compound wore an ID. In today's world of computers and microchips the issued ID was laughable. It was a green, cardboard card, with a place for a picture and captioned

"Unlimited Access." Filled out by hand and laminated with plastic, we wore it around our necks, suspended by a small chain.

If a valid witness was identified, we took a statement and then made sure he was present for the trial. I can't remember if we did subpoenas or merely requested that he be brought to court. The U.S. Attorney's office ensured the presence of their witnesses.

I won't ever forget one investigation. The facts of the case itself are long forgotten. but where Gus and I found the witness was memorable. He was located in the upstairs of his barracks near his bunk. Hanging from the ceiling and bedposts were what appeared to be balloons. A closer inspection revealed that they were actually condoms that had been inflated and hung from the ceiling by colored ribbons. It must have been quite a party.

The barracks were also decorated with art. The Cubans are a very artistic people—and they had a lot of time on their hands. In fact, one of my satisfied clients presented me with wall hanging that he had made.

The refugees were also resourceful. They could make a weapon out of most anything as revealed when the raid after the breakout produced many handmade weapons. Someone told me that either the Special Forces or CIA sent a team to Chaffee to inspect the confiscated weapons.

Assistant U.S. Attorney Neal Kirkpatrick prosecuted these cases. As noted by Judge Holmes in his interview, Neal took this work very seriously and personally. An early issue we dealt with on a regular basis was the age of the younger detainees. If they were younger than 16, it made a difference in where they were housed and how they were charged.

We were milling around in the old army office building we were using as a court one day—and Neal, who

I had known since he was in high school, was talking with one of the law enforcement Officers when I joined the conversation. The topic was the age of a defendant who claimed to be a juvenile. Neal was saying that they were going to have a dentist check his teeth for wear like they do for horses in order to determine age. I probably laughed. Neal turned and ordered me to walk away as they were discussing trial strategy. All I could think of was "Never look a gift Cuban in the mouth." This is not the last time Neal Kirkpatrick got perturbed.

In early December or late November of 1980, a new person joined the cast of characters. Captain Leo Martinez was a JAG officer and very good lawyer and bilingual as well. The army had actually sent him to law school. He became the new special associate U.S. attorney relieving Neal of the day-to-day operations of La Corte del Magistrado. Leo was later replaced by another JAG officer, Captain Dan Dell'Orto. Neal retained the duties of trying felony cases that he later shared with the other AUSAs in the office.

U.S. Magistrate Ned Stewart, Jr., grateful for the establishment of my position, wrote a letter January 6, 1981, addressed to Senators Bumpers and Pryor and Congressman Hammerschimdt concerning the situation at Fort Chaffee regarding the Cubans. Senator Bumpers placed this letter into the Congressional Record:

> *During the past several months, I have been heavily engaged in conducting misdemeanor court proceedings at Fort Chaffee involving Cuban refugee defendants. Since the inception o f our court proceedings at Fort Chaffee in June of this past year, we have handled approximately 625 refugee defendants through my court. This is an unusually high volume of cases considering that none of the refugee defendants spoke English nor had any familiarity whatsoever with our judicial system.*

It would have been virtually impossible for me to handle this volume of cases through my court but for the considerable assistance I have received from other federal agencies and employees engaged in law enforcement activities at Fort Chaffee. Many of these agencies and employees are no longer at Fort Chaffee, having been returned to their regular duty roles and stations. Although all of the assistance rendered me has been good, some has been particularly good to the end that, in my judgment, it is worthy of special praise and recognition. As all of you are directly concerned with Fort Chaffee, I thought it appropriate to call these matters to your attention.

Up until recently, the United States Park Police has had the principal responsibility for law enforcement within the refugee compound. This agency has recently been replaced in this regard by the Federal Protective Service. During their stay at Fort Chaffee the Park Police did an outstanding job under what can only be described as very difficult conditions. While all the Park Police I encountered did their jobs in a professional and competent manner, there are three individuals associated with this agency that I would like to single out for special praise: Detective Pat Moyer, U.S. Park Police, Washington, D.C.; Detective Louis Robinson, U.S. Park Police, Washington, D. C.; and Mr. Raul Jiminez, Park Police interpreter, shortly to be associated, I believe, with the Puerto Rico State Police, San Juan, Puerto Rico. These three individuals were directly concerned with my court operations on a day to day basis and rendered invaluable services to my court on many, many occasions. I cannot praise these men too highly.

We now have in place at Fort Chaffee solely in support of the court proceedings involving refugee defendants a temporary Federal Public Defender office. Because of the high volume of refugee defendants going through my court, this office has proved crucial to the success of my court proceedings. When I requested the establishment of this office several months ago, I was fearful the administrative requirements would delay its establishment considerably if, indeed, it could be established at all. Mr. Norman Lynch, Chief, Criminal Justice Act Division, Administrative Office of the U. S. Courts, Washington, D.C. and Mr. Ray Conrad, Federal Public Defender, Kansas City, Missouri, came to my aid in this regard and established this temporary office in record time. I very much appreciate the special efforts put forth by these two men.

We also now have a place at Fort Chaffee a special prosecutor assigned to my court, a Captain Leo Martinez, Judge Advocate General Corps, U. S. Army. In addition to being an able officer and lawyer, Captain Martinez is bilingual and performs exceptionally well in my court on this account. Captain Martinez was made available to serve in my court through the special efforts of Mr. Larry McCord, U.S. Attorney, Fort Smith, and General Hugh R. Overholt, Judge Advocate General Corps, Washington, D. C. A very good example of mutually beneficial civilian-military cooperation.

Finally, I must give special commendation to my secretary, Mrs. Janie Gazzola, and my court interpreter, Mrs. Rachael Smith. Both of these ladies have worked long arduous hours under difficult conditions and done truly a superior job. Mrs. Smith, by the way is the wife of a Fort Smith attorney, Mr. Don Smith, and is not a full time government employee. She has served my court at considerable sacrifice to her family life.

I very much appreciate your taking time out of your busy schedule to consider my comments. I feel strongly that the agencies and individuals mentioned above are most deserving of whatever recognition this letter might afford them.

Yours very truly.

Ned A. Stewart, Jr.

VII

CONSOLIDATION

THE SITUATION AND LONGEVITY of the Fort Chaffee operation became more acute in September 1980, when the military announced that Chaffee would become the consolidation facility for the other bases that were ready to be shut down as more and more Cubans found sponsors and left the custody of the federal government.

A story in the SWTR by Kevin Laval on September 26, announced their arrival. It said that an estimated seven thousand refugees from the other bases were being moved to Chaffee to join the three thousand remaining here. That was a drastic reduction from the June total of eighteen thousand at Chaffee alone at the time of the riot. A great many detainees were released to sponsors within three months of arrival. About six hundred were moved from Eglin, AFB to allow for closing that facility along with twenty-five hundred each from Fort Indiantown Gap, PA, and Fort McCoy, WI. Note that the numbers don't add up to seven thousand. That meant that the population of Chaffee would be close to nine thousand. Among these individuals were those deemed most difficult to find sponsors—the mentally ill, homosexuals, criminals and others considered undesirable and hard to place. Thirty-nine of the new arrivals were placed in Level II, a highly-guarded and fenced area for the most dangerous. Again the storyline put out by the authorities was overly optimistic. They believed that the relocation center would shut down as soon as the end of 1980. It would not close until February of 1982.

On October 26, the U.S. Marshals Service replaced the U.S. Park Police as the policing entity for Chaffee and the refugees. The Park Police mainly stationed in Washington, D.C. and were needed for the upcoming presidential inauguration in January.[1]

---

1   Kevin Laval, Southwest Times Record, vol. 90 #96, September 26, 1980

VIII

OUR USUAL BUSINESS

TYPICAL CHARGES FOR THE detainees were assault, theft, marijuana sale and possession. There were also public sex acts, deviant sex acts and prostitution. There was just about anything one could imagine—and some things one couldn't imagine—going on among this group of people, some with dubious backgrounds, confined behind fencing and barbed wire with nothing much to do.

Among the material that Rachael Smith retained were some actual charging documents along with daily dockets. A review of them reveals the type of cases and activities that were going on inside the compound.

The docket for November 4, 1980, had twelve names:

• Jorge Valiente Gonzales, charged with theft, requested a lawyer.

• Felipe Tejara Hernandez, charged with theft, requested a lawyer.

• Luis Gonzales Elsia, charged with assault, requested a lawyer.

• Raul Catalino Cantun Carrera, charged with assault, requested a lawyer.

- Jorge Rodriquiz Laborit, charged with assault, requested a lawyer.

- William Ramos Echavarria, charged with marijuana possession and possession of a prohibited knife, requested a lawyer.

The others were all charged with assault and had not at that time requested a lawyer. The charging documents are revealing. The system was overloaded and many crimes that could have been charged as felonies were not. They were charged as misdemeanors because it would have really overloaded the system otherwise and caused much delay.

For example, Gerardo Font de Villa Valdez was charged with theft and the charge read as follows:

That on or about October 29, 1980, at Fort Chaffee, Arkansas, a place within the special or maritime jurisdiction of the United States in the Western District of Arkansas, Gerardo Font de Villa Valdez, A24791597 (his identification number), did commit an act of assault against Arcenio Hill Gonzales A24784494 by threatening him with a machete and putting him in fear for his life, in violation of 18 USC 113(e), and take and carry away with the intent to steal or purloin one radio cassette player along with six other radios, the property belonging to Arcenio Hill Gonzales and having a value of less than $100, in violation of 18 USC661.

That was actually a robbery and the property was more valuable than claimed. It could have been charged as a felony.

Sometimes there was even a bit of humor.

On December 5, 1980 Raymundo Fernandez Peres was charged with "knowingly obtain the property of another, to wit: Currency belonging to

U.S.Park Police Detective Patrick Hanley, by deception, with the purpose of depriving the owner thereof, in violation of 18 USC 13 and Ark. Stat. Ann. 41-2203 (b).

This genius was stealing from the cops! It seems he told the detective that he knew where there was a pistol on base and that he could get it for $15. The detective gave him the $15 to buy the gun in a controlled buy with marked money. Instead of purchasing the gun while the detectives looked on, he took the money and left and did not make any attempt at buying the gun. They caught him five buildings away. His next stop was the stockade.

Many of the charges faced by the refugees had to do with marijuana. They certainly weren't growing it and they didn't bring it with them—so where did it come from? It came from the outside, of course. People working on the base brought it in and sold it to the Cubans on the black market. It was just another boost to the local economy as a result of the Cuban Relocation Project.

We also had our share of mentally ill folks and those with a sex obsession. Andres Batancourt Castro was one of these individuals. He terrorized female employees and visitors. He was charged with assaulting a female employee on three different days in March of 1981. The victimized lady described sitting in a parked government vehicle when Batancourt approached. When he exposed his penis and placed it against her window, she attempted to get away—but Batancourt held the door shut. She yelled for help and he ran away. The FPS was not able to locate him at that time. A few days later this same lady and a female friend saw him standing at the bottom of some stairs holding a newspaper. As they approached, he moved the newspaper exposing his penis, and began masturbating. He fled once more before authorities could get there. On another day, this same lady was entering a building when Batancourt approached and asked her if she was his friend. She told him she did not make friends with "Chicken Chokers." (a term used for those who masturbated in public) When Batancourt announced he was going to "Chicken Choke" for her, she turned to leave—and Batancourt grabbed her by the buttocks. She hit him with her pocket book and kicked him causing him to leave. She gave the following description: white male, between 5'7" and 5'8" approximately 130 lbs with sunken cheeks, no teeth and wearing a green ball cap. He was located and positively identified.

This reminds me of a story I was told about a visit we had from the ACLU. They were making sure these folks were not being mistreated. A similar incident happened to that lady as the one Batancourt assaulted. She left and we did not hear from them again until the INS controversy.

The misdemeanor cases we handled at Chaffee were somewhat like a metaphor of life. The general population was in a cage surrounded by barbed wire. We all have our limitations and are in something of a cage. When the Cubans screwed up and were convicted, they were placed in a smaller cage surrounded by barbed wire called a stockade. When anyone screws up, they limit the size of their cage as well. Such is life.

IX

ATTICUS FINCH REDUX

IN THE SAME MONTH I went to work as the public defender, there was a disturbance or uprising among the refugees in Level II. This area was fully chain-link fenced to a height of about 12' topped with concertina wire. It was reserved for the problematic individuals suspected of being troublemakers.

The relative quiet at the fort was disrupted by a disturbance in the Level II area on October 7, 1980, that left eight persons injured. One INS officer had to have fourteen stitches. Four other officers and three refugees were also injured. The disturbance began when a Cuban struck a detention officer. The officer was searching for the Cuban inside a recreation hall. The officer said the Cuban had several items stuffed in his shirt and he was checking to see if they were "unauthorized." When he started the search, the Cuban took a swing at him and about twenty or thirty others swarmed the scene. The Cuban that struck the officer also hit him over the head with a chair. Other officers arrived on the scene and the disturbance was over in about five minutes. The refugee involved had recently been transferred to Chaffee from Fort McCoy, Wisconsin. Testimony at the trial would be a bit different from the facts stated in the news article.[1]

---

1   Molly Palmer, *Southwest Times Record,* vol. 87 # 282 October 9, 1980

Allegations of abuse of the refugees by members of the INS and park police started coming to the fore in about July and had resulted in investigations. The editor of the SWTR, Jack Moseley, in a front-page story on October 18, 1980, entitled 'Brutality charged at Chaffee,' stated that accusations of excessive force had been leveled at employees of the two federal agencies with complaints coming from both military and civilian sources. The SWTR confirmed that a complaint was made to the American Red Cross two weeks earlier.

Someone subsequently contacted the paper about a twenty-one-year-old detainee who suffered a broken jaw. A guard reportedly hit the young man while he stood in the food line reaching for a piece of meat. Following medical treatment, the young man attempted suicide rather than return to the base. He was fearful of additional injury. The INS said no one knew how the young man was injured. He required surgery and was terrified of the INS guard who accompanied him to the hospital. Other refugees in Level II told of being stripped naked and tied to their bunks. One guard was referred to as "Mr. Death." The restrained individuals had to ask permission to even go to the bathroom. They had to keep their heads down at all times. The refugees stated they would kill "Mr. Death" if they ever got the chance. There were reports of refugees having bruising in the groin area. The U.S. Park Police were implicated by reports of more force than necessary being used in arrests for minor offenses.[2]

Into this mix of violence and allegations of abuse, I was appointed to represent Elipido Munteliel-Galan on an indictment for assault that was returned on October 31, 1980. This was the first time I represented a Cuban on a felony charge. The charge grew from the disturbance on October 7, which had been the subject of Molly Palmer's story. My client was the instigator of

2 Jack Moseley, *Southwest Times Record,* vol. 87 # 292, October 18, 1980

the whole affray according to the INS. It was for this reason and the fact that the victim was an officer that he was charged with a felony instead of a misdemeanor as were many other simple assault cases.

INMATE IN THE BLOCKADE

U.S. District Judge G. Thomas Eisele received the assignment. Following the indictment, I appeared with my client before Judge Eisele on November 5, and entered a plea of not guilty. A trial was set for November 18. Motions were filed including those by me for inspection of the case and for discovery and a motion by the government for disclosure of evidence and to discover whether the defendant had an alibi.

This is all pretty routine stuff. I did know, however, that the FBI conducted an investigation into the whole affair. I filed a motion to change the venue of the case outside of Fort Smith due to the negative publicity and news coverage of the Cuban refugees. Both PK Holmes and Gene Wahl had filed similar motions in the cases assigned to them and heard by Judge Williams. None were successful.

On November 19, 1980, there was a hearing before Judge Eisele on all motions including the change of venue. I called local attorney Bob Blatt to tell of the feelings in the legal community on the possibility of seating an impartial jury; local radio personality Fred Baker, Jr. to tell of the sentiments in the community regarding the refugees and editor of the SWTR, Jack Moseley who had been subpoenaed along with the multitude of stories from the paper concerning the refugees and the problems they caused or encountered. I recall that Jack was somewhat hostile to me because I caused him to bring all those stories and lug them to court. It was a real inconvenience to say the least and I was not the only attorney to have him do this. He was tired of going to court. Judge Eisele took the motion under advisement and to the surprise of everyone he granted it and set the matter for trial in the U. S. Courthouse in Hot Springs.

The trial was set for December 29, 1980. The matter proceeded in an unremarkable way but the testimony was different than the newspaper article in early October. The government's star witness and the only person who could identify Elpidio was an INS detention officer named Larry Ferrell who worked in the recreation hall where the incident occurred. He was the projector operator. He testified that a movie was about to start. Elpidio, unprovoked, jumped up and yelled "Cuba Libre!" or "Libertad!" and struck him with his fist. Then a mini riot broke out. This was not consistent with the news story about a refugee being searched. I knew something that Neal Kirkpatrick, the assistant U.S. attorney, and the witness didn't know. This knowledge made the difference in the outcome of the case. The reader will recall Harper Lee's novel "To Kill a Mockingbird." The protagonist in the story was a young girl called Scout. Her father, Atticus Finch, played by Gregory Peck in the movie was an attorney. He defended a young black man named Tom Robinson who was wrongly accused of raping a white girl. The girl maintained that Tom held her with his left arm during the attack. Atticus confronted her with the fact that Tom's left arm was paralyzed. It made no difference in the novel. Tom was convicted. In talking with Elpidio in the stockade I noticed he had trouble with his right hand. He told me it had been paralyzed as a result of a knife fight in jail in Cuba. All the tendons in his wrist had been severed. The hand was basically useless.

When I got Mr. Ferrell on cross examination I asked him, "You tell me my client hit you with his hand is that correct?"

"Yes, sir", he responded.

"Can you explain to me exactly how this occurred?" He hesitated a moment and I interjected, "Did he hit you with his fist?" My voice was getting louder and I approached with my right fist clenched.

"Yes!" he responded, his voice rising.

"Was it his right fist just like this?"

"Yes!" There was a little desperation in his voice.

"So he jumped up, cried 'Cuba Libre" and struck you with his right fist doubled up. Is that your testimony?" I spoke loudly and maintained eye contact.

"Yes," he responded.

"No question in your mind?"

"No." He was almost yelling.

My voice dropped low and I said, "Would it surprise you to know that his right hand is paralyzed?"

He had stepped into my trap. Going in I had no idea what his testimony was going to be. If he had said left hand, my client was screwed. Of course, I did help suggest it was his right as I had that fist clenched as I questioned him.

I put my client on the stand to deny the charges and to show, that indeed, his right hand was paralyzed. He claimed he was only protecting himself during the melee. The trial for all intents and purposes was over at that time. The witness' credibility was in doubt.

Neal objected vehemently and tried to rehabilitate the witness. He even recalled an FBI agent to say the open palm could be a lethal weapon but it was no avail. In my closing to the jury I reminded them that the world was watching what was happening in Fort Chaffee and today in Hot Springs, Arkansas. Not only was my client on trial but also was America. America is the paragon of justice for all and it means all. Even Elpidio Mustelier Galan, someone who had been maimed in a jail fight in Cuba was entitled to American justice where the charges had to be proven beyond a reasonable doubt. Anyway it was words to that effect.

The jury agreed and acquitted my client. What had not worked for Atticus Finch worked for me. Facts overcame prejudice. Phil Moomaw second chaired me in the trial and I passed his scrutiny.

Feeling pretty good about myself, I thanked each of the jurors as they filed out. One lady stopped and said, "With no help from you! You are too arrogant and smug young man! You just leaned back in your chair the whole time the other side was talking!"

I guess she put me in my place. But it was my best time as a trial lawyer.

X

THE INS TRIAL

THE MATTER OF THE riot at the movie was not over. More drama was to ensue.

On January 14, 1981, Jack Moseley wrote an article about an ongoing grand jury investigation into allegations of excessive force used against Level II refugees at Fort Chaffee. Federal employees who first reported the matter, afraid of retaliation, were effectively silenced.

The initial report by the FBI found no civil rights violations or brutality. The U.S. Park Police and INS investigations were ongoing, however. Some of the incidents predated the movie incident that involved my client Muntelier-Galan.

The INS made no comments. The abuse allegations listed beatings, groin kicks—and refugees stripped and tied to their bunks. Moseley noted that it would be difficult to obtain indictments as it would be the word of the refugees housed in the section for the most unruly and the word of federal officers.

An unnamed source gave Mr. Moseley a good and prescient quote:

If brutality has been used against Cubans that is a horrible thing. The only positive thing that can be said about that is that we live in a country that will investigate the charges with the full force of laws designed to protect people, not persecute them. That at least must be encouraging to people like these refugees who have lived so long under Communism. The beautiful thing about our system is that it is strong enough to permit investigations like those now underway. And if facts warrant, I am sure our own government will move to see that justice is done.[1]

Facts evidently warranted because the Civil Rights division of the U.S. Department of Justice ordered a new investigation on January 1, 1981. In October, the workers who made the initial complaints would not talk to the investigators out of fear of losing their jobs. Now, with DOJ civil rights division investigators involved, this evidently changed.[2]

Bilingual investigators were brought in to talk with the refugees. On May 27, 1981, the federal grand jury returned indictments against five INS officers. The charges included seventeen counts of brutality against Cuban refugees along with one count of conspiracy said to have occurred in Level II in September and October of 1980. Those charged as co-conspirators and perpetrators were: INS supervisor detention officer Curtis Clark of Elk Grove, Illinois, and guards Wayne Richardson of Denver, Colorado, James Lane of Brooklyn, New York, Jimmy Davis of Yuma, Arizona and Eugene Palleschi of Brooklyn, New York.[3]

Clark was the alleged instigator. Supposedly, he instructed his subordinates on the night shifts to beat the Cubans being processed into the Level II area. He then demonstrated his instructions by striking a refugee with a riot baton—and then ordering two other guards to strike a refugee with the same baton.

1   Jack Moseley, *Southwest Times Record*, vol. 91 #14, January 14, 1981
2   Jack Moseley, *Southwest Times Record*, vol. 91 # 16, January 16, 1981
3   Jenny Deam, *Southwest Times Record*, vol. 91 # 148,May 28, 1981

RIOT AT FORT CHAFFEE

Clark's charges included an incident where he had the refugees in Barracks 1334 stripped and tied or hand-cuffed to their bunks. This was to punish them for their participation in a disturbance arising during the showing of a movie. *The Southwest Times Record* reported that during this episode, the detainees were forced to keep their heads down and ask permission to get a drink, use the restroom, eat or smoke.

Clark was also accused of ordering another officer to erase documentation of alleged abuse from a refugee's medical records. The charges enumerated specific incidents by victim and perpetrator. The indictment stated that the defendants conspired to assault Cuban detainees with dangerous weapons such as riot batons, slappers (leather paddles with a lead weight in the end), and shod feet with the intention of inflicting bodily harm.

Richardson and Lane were said to have introduced themselves to the refugees as "Official de la Muerta"(Officer of Death) and "El Planadora"(the Steamroller) in an attempt to elicit fear.

The grand jury met in December and again in February and April before returning indictments in May. U.S. Attorney General William French Smith said that the charges resulted from a six month investigation by the FBI, the INS office of professional responsibility, and the Justice Department of Professional Responsibility. Smith said:

The immigration service's internal investigation reflects great credit on that organization's ability to investigate fairly allegations involving its own personnel.[4]

In June, the defendants were placed on administrative leave with pay and later suspended without pay. The salaries ranged from $23,000 for Clark, a supervisor, to

4   Deam, ibid

$12,600 for Richardson. The rate of pay is an indication of the cost of living in 1981.[5]

The defendants entered not guilty pleas on May 31, 1981. Eddie Christian represented all the defendants except Clark who was represented by a lawyer from Chicago, Ronald Rascia. Daniel Bell and Criselda Ortiz represented the United States. They were attorneys with the USDOJ civil rights division. The case was set for September. [6]

Defendant Clark changed attorneys. His new lawyer was Charles Karr of Fort Smith, a former prosecuting attorney. The trial got underway on September 14, with opening arguments.

Eddie Christian insisted that the actions described in the charges were necessary to maintain discipline. He said:

Make no mistake about it there was some head-knocking and tail kicking but the evidence will show that in each and every instance it was deserved.

The defense maintained that there was no discipline before Curtis Clark took control of the day shift and the area was plagued with refugee uprisings. He brought the situation under control according to Mr. Karr.[7]

Daniel Bell argued that the defendants beat the refugees almost daily—and without provocation. The indictment described Clark striking a refugee and then instructing his subordinates to do the same. Bell said "the defendants ruled the area with systematic fear and violence." The defendants took the law into their own hands, assaulting the detainees scores of times.

5   Washington Bureau, *Southwest Times Record*, vol. 91#182, June 1, 1981
6   Jenny Deam, *Southwest Times Record*, vol. 91 #182, June 1, 1981
7   Jenny Deam, *Southwest Times Record*, vol. 91 #258, September 15, 1981

Ms. Deam noted that each defendant seemed nervous and grim faced.[8]

The first witness, Carl Gaglia, a supervisory detention officer on night shift, described observing Clark strike a refugee twice while he was being processed into the area. Clark then commanded other officers to follow his example. Gaglia stated that he objected but was threatened with a reprimand if he complained.

On Tuesday, refugees and detention officers again testified about the violence inflicted upon those being processed into Level II. Detainees identified Clark as the man they knew as "Senor Official" and the one who struck them.

Israel Torres, a refugee who had been sponsored out to Detroit, said Clark demanded to be addressed as "Senor Official" and threatened to hit them if they failed to do so. He said Clark hit them anyway even if they followed instructions. Torres remembered being slapped repeatedly.

Kenneth Linicome and Guadalupe Castro, former INS agents, expressed concern with the treatment of the incoming refugees. Curtis Clark ignored their protests. According to Linicome, Clark stated:

We'll get everyone involved and no one will know anything about it. It's not going to change so if you want to report it, report it.

INS officer Leon Bellamy, a former Clark subordinate, demonstrated how Clark poked refugees with riot batons while instructing them on how to answer questions. He saw refugee Torres beaten to his knees and kicked on September 23, 1980, despite his answering "Si Senor." He also saw a refugee with his arm in a cast lying at the foot of a barracks stair with Clark standing over him with a can of Mace.

8   Deam, ibid

On cross-examination, Bellamy admitted that the refugees were impossible to process and that repeated weapon sweeps consistently uncovered homemade knives.[9]

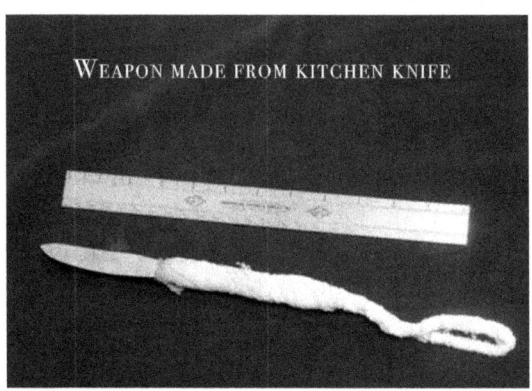

WEAPON MADE FROM KITCHEN KNIFE

The next day, the jury heard of a torture chamber. Lorenzo Perez Tomayo, a refugee who had been sponsored to New York, described being stripped naked and beaten as punishment for trying to escape. Taken to Level II after the failed attempt, seven officers beat Perez and another refugee:

They brought us back down and ordered us to take our clothes off. We were put on a white line and then they began to beat me and hit me in my head and other parts of my body.

Perez referred to the room used for processing as a torture chamber. Riot batons and slappers were used on him. He said Curtis Clark was present and threatened him with death if he told anyone of the incident.

Ruben Valez, a former interpreter at the medical unit, described Perez being brought to the clinic on a stretcher, badly beaten with imprints on his abdomen similar to slapper marks.

9 Jenny Deam, *Southwest Times Record*, vol. 91 #259, September 16, 1981

Larry Payne, an INS detention officer, heard "fearful screaming" from the area used for processing. Although he never witnessed the actual processing procedure, he understood that indiscriminate violence was used to keep refugees under control.[10]

The paper headlined next day's testimony with:

Officer claims refugees roughed up.

Raul Sepulveda, an INS officer on duty during the movie incident in October, told of eighty refugees storming him and six other officers. Following the incident, Sepulveda said that all suspected instigators were beaten by INS officers in an attempt to gain information. Sepulveda said:

They were roughed up. They were hit with riot batons and threatened unless they identified the instigators

When one refugee identified some of the others, guards herded the detainees into a corner, beat them further and sprayed them with Mace. Sepulveda described how they were handcuffed face down in their bunks.

Another witness, Armando Ochoa, who had been identified as one of the principals in the uprising, identified the defendants as the ones who beat him. Ochoa said that Clark told them he was going to "cleanse up by punishment our sins of the previous day."

Ralph Paige, who was with the INS Office of Professional Responsibility, testified that the investigation was sparked by complaints made by a hospitalized refugee assaulted by a detention officer.[11]

The following day two detention officers identified Curtis Clark, their former supervisor, as the one who kicked and Maced an injured refugee as he lay at the

10 Jenny Deam, *Southwest Times Record*, vol. 91 #260, September 17, 1981
11 Jenny Deam, *Southwest Times Record*, vol. 91 #261, September 18, 1981

foot of a barracks' stair. The refugee was named Jorge Luis Dominguez. Officer Michael Jolly of Boston said Clark ordered the refugee to stand. When he didn't, Clark kicked Dominguez, yanked him to his feet by his hair—and sprayed his face and genitals with Mace.

Jolly intervened, suggesting that the Cuban could not stand because his arm was in a Cast.

Clark responded, He's faking it!"

While they were walking Luis back to the barracks, Clark asked for Jolly's can of Mace and sprayed Luis three times with increasing intensity in the face and genitals. After Jolly wiped the Mace from the refugee and bedded him down in the barracks, Clark dragged the refugee out for a second time and, according to Jolly, "Maced him again."

After Clark left, Ernest Koch, an INS agent, handcuffed the refugee in an upright position in his bunk. Since Domenguez was on a hunger strike to protest his treatment, Koch tried to force feed him. This was unsuccessful.[12]

The following days brought more of the same type testimony. More refugees and INS officers identified the five defendants as the ones responsible for mistreatment. Most of this was an attempt to gain information on the uprising at the movie theater.

This only reaffirmed my thoughts in the Muntiellier trial that the authorities had no idea as to the cause and parties responsible for the uprising at the movie. During three hour of cross-examination, Jorge Luis Perez Dominguez wavered. First, he identified other refugees to the officers as the ones involved in the uprising in order to shield himself from further abuse—and then he said he didn't. He denied taking part in the melee. He testified that he merely climbed out a window and was later injured by a blow that broke his arm. He said that

12   Jenny Deam, *Southwest Times Record*, vol. 91 # 262, September 19,1981

he began his hunger strike at the clinic. After four days
Clark came to the clinic and ordered him out and threw
him on the ground. Clark and another officer tried to
force feed him. In order to get him to open his mouth,
Curtis Clark punched him while another officer held a
riot baton across his chest. This attempt to get him to
eat failed and he was left on the ground for two hours.[13]

Following motions the next day, the defense succeeded in having some of the charges thrown out. Two
of the eighteen counts of conspiracy were dismissed as
not being proven to the extent that it should go to the
jury.[14]

The headline in the SWTR on September 25
was,"Defense rests in INS trial."

Two of the defendants testified that if they had it
all to do over again they would do the same thing. Jimmy Davis and Wayne Richardson echoed each other.
"I never worked out on any refugee!" Davis stated on
cross-examination. In the instance of the uprising on
October 7, 1980, when the movie was being shown he
stated, "They were throwing anything they could get
their hands on." He was even struck by a flying portion
of the movie projector.

Davis admitted that guards struck refugees during
and after the Disturbance. However, he maintained that
any force used was discipline. Davis denied that the day
after the disturbance, the defendants were stripped and
randomly beaten in order to obtain information.

Davis said:

*Any refugee that was struck was a defensive
blow when they attacked an officer. The aliens
were fighting and spitting and acting like fools.
I thought, 'my God, it's the (June 1) riot all
over again.*

13 Jenny Deam, *Southwest Times Record*, vol. 91 # 265, September 22, 1981
14 Jenny Deam, *Southwest Times Record*, vol. 91 #266, September 23, 1981

Richardson testified:

As far as beatings, there were no beatings. Discipline yes. They wee like a bunch of wild kids; without discipline they would just go wild.

Richardson laughingly admitted that he was nicknamed "Official de la muerte" which means officer of death. He said that came from his inability to speak fluent Spanish. He told the refugees not to cause any disturbances because if a riot broke out some Cubans might "visit with death." He said he did introduce himself as Official de la muerte for purposes of intimidation. He was 6' 1" and weighed 225. Intimidation can be useful for control.[15]

On September 29, the headline read 'Fate of five officers rests with jury.'

On Monday, the closing arguments and instructions lasted two hours. The jury started its deliberations on Tuesday morning. Criselda Ortiz closed for the government and recounted testimony...

...refugees in Level II were systematically, routinely, and as a matter of daily practice, physically assaulted by the defendants. Defendant Clark would sic the security guards on the refugees like a pack of wild dogs. That was the welcome these refugees got to our country.

Charles Karr, the attorney for Curtis Clark, told the jury that the defendants had a duty to maintain control. Whatever they did was in performance of their duty. He reminded the jury that the refugees in Level II were violence oriented and therefore the guards had to use some force to maintain order.

15   Jenny Deam, *Southwest Times Record*, vol. 91 #268, September 25, 1981

From the very beginning I think this (The Cuban Relocation Project) has been the biggest bureaucratic bungle ever. With all that happened out there, to single out and try to make scapegoats out of these men...to do that is perhaps the greatest miscarriage of justice in this century.

Eddie Christian, the attorney for the other defendants, reminded jurors of the Federal government's promise to Arkansas that they would bring no criminals into Chaffee. The promise, he said, was broken.

Did they (referring to the prosecution) bring you the whole truth or is it just another broken promise? The disciplinary methods used by the defendants were no different than a Marine boot camp! There was some head-knocking and tail kicking but it wasn't anymore than needed to be done.

Daniel Bell closing for the government in rebuttal discounted the defense arguments saying, "They are just like an octopus giving off black ink to cloud the issues." [16]

The jury started its deliberations on Tuesday and went until 5:45 p.m. At their request, the case was recessed until Wednesday morning.

"You have been working hard, and I know that you're tired. You've been at it all day long," Judge Harris told them.

The jury foreman replied, "We've made progress but we have further to go than we have gone all day."

At the end of the day on Wednesday, the jury still had not reached a verdict on all counts.

Judge Harris asked the jury foreman if they were making progress.

---

16   Mike Crowden, *Southwest Times Record*, vol. 91 #272, September 29, 1981

"That depends on the definition of progress," the foreman responded, "Yes, on some counts we have—but on some counts, we have reached the conclusion that we are at an impasse."

Before dismissing the jury for the nigh, Judge Harris said, "This is a most important case and it needs to be decided...I'm very anxious that the jury, in its deliberation, comes to a conclusion."

After the jury departed, the judge told the lawyers that when Court resumed, he intended to give the jury "the Allen type instruction," which is sometimes called "the dynamite charge." That is, while the jury must not to go against their consciences in making their decision, they should be open-minded to any arguments other jurors may offer. The judge will mention the expense of the trial, estimated to be about $200,000.00. Harris also told the lawyers, "I'm going to suggest to you to be thinking if a partial verdict would be acceptable...to me it would not."[17]

However, that is exactly what they got. On Friday, the jury came in with not guilty verdicts on thirteen of the twenty-seven counts. Judge Harris declared a mistrial on the one remaining count.

I have a report that the jury reached an impasse. Having reached this stage in the proceedings, I am greatly disappointed. But nothing can be done about it...I'm going to ask that you turn in the decisions that you have reached a unanimous decision on. The government has seventy days to decide whether it will seek to try again any or all of the defendants on the charges left undecided by the jury.

17 Mike Crowden, *Southwest Times Record*, vol. 91 #273, October 1, 1981

The defendants were overjoyed–and they hugged and cheered. Asked to comment, one of the defendants said, "How 'bout them Hogs!"[18]

The government decided to retry the case on the remaining charges. John Wilson, the assistant director of professional responsibility for the Department of Justice stated, "We don't do things lightly, if we believe there are valid charges originally, then they are still valid."

Daniel Bell, one of the attorneys who tried the case for the government said, "It's the best judgment of the department that the evidence is strong and merits a retrial."[19]

The government was tiring of the Cubans and all the added work for the understaffed personnel. Speaking to the Rotary Club, William Kell, the FBI agent, said they would be relieved when the refugees were removed from western Arkansas. He reported that since the Cubans arrived in May of 1980, the FBI had investigated one hundred and two felony complaints including three homicide cases and of these only nineteen resulted in convictions. While all three homicides received convictions, Kell was critical of Judge Paul X. Williams' sentences. A jury reduced one murder case to manslaughter.

"Human life is a very cheap commodity in the Federal court in western Arkansas," Kell told the Rotarians. Many cases were dismissed due to mental illness. He complained about the investigation into the June 1, 1980, riot being slow and tedious with numerous interviews. Many times the victims refused to identify the assailants. Kell described the FBI role as "...one of the most frustrating undertakings we've ever had."[20]

The government's frustration with its own legal system was apparent when called upon to prosecute its own

18   Mike Crowden, *Southwest Times Record*, vol. 91 #276, October 3, 1981
19   John Wilson, *Southwest Times Record*, vol. 91 #295, October 22, 1981
20   Mike Crowden, *Southwest Times Record*,

officers. The retrial got underway in early December.[21]
The testimony was a repeat of the earlier trial. Refugee Armando Ochoa told of Richardson beating him
following the uprising at the movie. The testimonies
of Clark as "The Director" and Lane as "The Steamroller" and Davis as "Second to Death," were repeated.
Several guards testified against their coworkers. The
defense pointed out inconsistencies in prior testimony.
The prosecution's case went on for the entire week and
into the next week. After the final government witness,
the defense moved for acquittal which was denied. This
was at the conclusion of the government's case.[22]

On Tuesday, after the jury had been dismissed Judge
Harris asked a question to which he could not get an
answer. He wanted to know exactly who was in charge
of security at Fort Chaffee when the five INS officers
allegedly abused Cuban refugees. He found out who
it was that supervised the officers but not who was in
charge of the overall operation. Judge Harris noted that
almost none of the witnesses had even heard of the Joint
Security Plan, which was formulated by the Justice and
Defense Departments to detail security responsibilities
among various agencies at Fort Chaffee. He noted that
the plan had seemingly been disregarded:

*I don't understand it. It gives me great concern on
behalf of both the refugees and these defendants.*

Mr. Bell had placed a copy of the management plan
into evidence. In the trial most of the officers testified
that they had received no formal training or written instructions on how to handle the refugees in Level II.
Curtis Clark told the jury that when he arrived at Chaffee in September, 1980, there were no established rules
or regulations for the refugees.[23]

21   Jane Nicholes, *Southwest Times Record*, vol. 91 #338, December 4, 1981
22   Jane Nicholes, *Southwest Times Record*, vol. 91 #'s 339 & 342, December 5&8, 1981
23   Jane Nicholes, *Southwest Times Record*, vol. 9 # 343, December 9, 1981

Retrial testimony ended on December 9, 1981. Judge Harris made a comment while the jury was out in conversation:

You can never tell when a mule will kick or what a jury will do.

This was telling.

Harris read his instructions and the lawyers made their closing arguments on Thursday.[24]

On December 12, the headline read:

Five INS officers found innocent; Judge Harris calls case 'a vivid lesson.

The jury was out less than eight hours and as the verdicts were read, three of the five defendants had tears in their eyes. Judge Harris stated:

I just hope and pray that this will be a vivid lesson to this country, that if this situation should ever arise again there will be better consideration given to the totality of it. It has been a hard case. It has throughout.

These words came during his message of thanks to the jury.

The defendants all shook hands and hugged as the judge dismissed them. Charles Karr, who represented Clark, wiped his eyes and stated:

We're extremely gratified. I just feel that this case should never have been brought in the first place.

Larry McCord the U.S. Attorney said:

24   Jane Nicholes, *Southwest Times Record*, vol. 91 # 344, December 10, 1981

Naturally we are disappointed, but we accept the verdict of the jury.

The two government lawyers from DC left the courtroom without comment. It was not a total loss for them however. Rachael Smith told me that the two had fallen in love and ended up getting married.

Jimmy Davis, one of the defendants said:

We did our job and the court did their job. That's about the size of it. It's justice.

Curtis Clark said:

I don't know what to say, we were innocent all the time.

Eddie Christian the attorney for all the defendants except Clark said:

I'm going duck hunting. The jury said it all.

And so it was all over. It had been a great financial burden on the men charged. One had to work two jobs during the period they were suspended without pay and sell his car to pay his fare back to Fort Smith for the second trial. They were unsure how they would respond to some the officers who testified against them in the future.[25]

This was not a frivolous case as the defendants expressed. The evidence was strong enough for a grand jury to indict Federal officers for abusing unsympathetic victims. The first trial jury was undecided after many hours of deliberations on some of the charges. Other officers testified against their comrades. That is powerful. Something happened in Level II. Judge Harris nailed it. The problem was that no one was in charge. That was the problem from the start at Fort Chaffee and the

---

25   Jane Nicholes, *Southwest Times Record*, vol. 91 # 346, December 12, 1981

Cuban situation. There was no one in charge. There was no one in charge at the start, at the June riot and into late 1980. How could anyone have prepared for this?

XI

OTHER FELONY CASES

DURING MY TIME AS the adjunct Federal Public Defender, I was assigned several felony cases. Elpidio was the first and the only one whose name I remember. Most were agreed guilty pleas and many of these were merely sentenced to time served. As noted, this was not pleasing to the FBI.

Others, the more serious, received sentences for terms of years. For example, Giraldo Martinez-Delgado was indicted for maiming on Feb. 18, 1981. The lawyers filed the usual motions and requested another hearing for a change of venue.

This was much as the case of Senor Mustelier-Galan but with a different result before Judge Williams. After changing his plea to guilty in April and following a pre-sentence report, he was sentenced to two years in prison with credit for time served which was about five months.

In one case the time served was in excess of the sentence imposed and the defendant was immediately released.

There were four cases of assault and all were handled similarly. There was one case of assault with intent to do bodily harm. Following the customary motions beginning with the indictment in May of 1981, the plea was changed to guilty and the sentence was time served.

There were two felony indictments for theft of a government vehicle. They were companion cases and the date of the indictment was July 29, 1981. Again lawyers filed all the proper motions. In September both changed their pleas to guilty and received a three-year probation to begin when they were sponsored out of the resettlement program.

There was one case of murder and a companion case of aiding and abetting in the murder. The defendant was Julio Beltran-Perez. The co-defendant was Ramon Cruz-Martinez. Cruz (the second name in Spanish culture is the surname) was accused of providing the weapon used in the killing. It was a .25 cal. pistol. Where it was originally obtained was never determined but it had to be brought in from the outside. The date of the indictment was February 18, 1981. I moved for a change of venue out of the district and a hearing was held on March 23, 1981. I called as witnesses: Jack Moseley, again, Davis Woods, a television reporter for channel 40, Kevin Laval a SWTR reporter and Steve Sharum a local attorney. I submitted affidavits from Harry Foltz the executive director of Western Arkansas Legal Services, Fred Baker, Jr. the radio personality and P.K. Holmes the attorney who had represented the refugees before the position I then held was created.

Despite all of this the motion was denied. I tried to get the cases severed for trial. This was denied but the government filed an amended charge against Senor Cruz and obviated the necessity of severing the case. Senor Beltran proceeded to trial.

The only defense was self-defense as there was no question Beltran had fired the fatal shot. He was a small individual and apparently not able to defend himself physically. As I recall, the deceased and his friends were terrorizing Beltran and he feared for his safety. I hoped this would be an emotional incentive for the jury to accept the self-defense argument. The argument proved somewhat successful as he was acquitted of the second degree murder charge but found guilty of voluntary manslaughter. Following the pre-sentence report he was sentenced to five years in the penitentiary. I moved for a reduction in the sentence that was denied. His co-defendant, Cruz, later pled guilty to his charges and received a sentence of three years in the penitentiary.

The final case I will discuss is that of co-defendants Osvaldo Fernandez-Fernandez and Santiago Malagon-Hernandez. They were charged with assault and assault to commit rape. The facts alleged were that the two defendants assaulted a young man and held him at bay while the two of them raped his girl friend.

The defense was that the girl and her boyfriend were lying so they would get the alleged attackers in trouble. It was a case of he and she said against he and he said. Physical evidence was scant. They were acquitted. This case I tried against AUSA Mike Fitzhugh with whom I later served many years as a circuit judge in Fort Smith.

As earlier stated most cases were guilty pleas as is the usual criminal court practice. Three felony cases were actually tried during my time as public defender. Two cases ended in acquittal and one a reduced charge. Not bad considering the defendants were Cuban refugees who were very unpopular in the community. I never missed an opportunity to argue to the juries that the good name of the United States was on trial along with the defendants and to not hold their status against them in their determinations. They never did. For this I am very proud of our citizens and the sense of duty and honor that they exhibited.

As a footnote to this section I believe that every one of the defendants I represented in a felony trial ended up in the Atlanta Federal Prison and were eventually returned to Cuba. The determination of the INS on their status had little to do with the fact they may have been acquitted of a criminal charge.

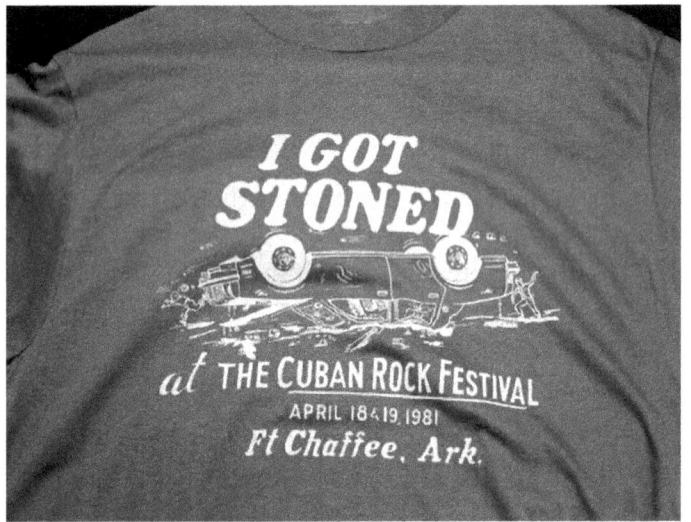

XII

THEN THEY WERE GONE

THE HEADLINE ON JANUARY 27, 1982, was simply
"Gone." The remaining refugees were being transferred
to Federal prisons in Springfield, Missouri and Atlanta,
Georgia. The exception was thirty individuals who were
sent to Seattle and Washington, D.C. for some special
programs. U.S. District Judge Marvin Shoob said it was
shameful and a tragedy that persons otherwise cleared
for release are being shipped off to maximum security prisons merely because sponsors could not be found
for them.

Some of my former clients filled these ranks even
those that had been acquitted. Governor Frank White
maintained it made little difference that they were sent
to a prison because "Fort Chaffee is a prison too."
He was correct. When one is kept behind a fence and
barbed wire that person is in a prison. It was anticipated that the entire operation would be shut down and
the six-hundred-person-civilian workforce out of work
within three weeks.[1]

On January 30, the SWTR carried a story about a
young woman and her daughter who had been born at
Fort Chaffee. The five-week- old girl was a U.S. citizen. The woman was not allowed to leave Cuba with her

1   Mike Crowden, *Southwest Times Record*, vol. 92 # 27, January 27, 1982

other two children, a five-year-old boy and a two-year -old girl. She left them with her mother and hoped they could be reunited again. Circumstances also separated her from her boyfriend and father of the baby. The government moved him to one of the prisons. She and the baby went to a hospital in another state so they could be together until moved again to Seattle, Washington. She expressed hope for her young daughter, Michelle. "I feel the baby will have a better life here than in Cuba."[2]

The headline on the front page of the February 4, 1982 SWTR read, "Last of Refugees leave Chaffee." They had left on a bus at 6:15 a.m. the previous morning, twenty-two of them, on their way to the Chicago Metropolitan Correctional Center.

It was over.

It was over for me as well. I knew it was temporary when I took the job but as I told the interviewer, I wanted to be a part of history. I certainly was.[3]

I had also hoped that it might turn into something permanent and I believed that might happen. The new U. S. Attorney was Asa Hutchinson, the present Governor of Arkansas. There was an opening on his staff and I applied. I believed with my experience in the Federal criminal system for over a year with some success I would have a leg up. It was not to be. Although I had a promising interview I was not selected and I was now among those whose job was lost due to the closing of the relocation center. At the end of February, I loaded my car up with all the papers, records and excess supplies that belonged to the Federal Public Defender and made my way to Kansas City to turn them in to Ray Conrad.

---

2   Mike Crowden, *Southwest Times Record,* vol. 92 # 30, January 30, 1982
3   *Southwest Times Record*, vol. 92 # 35, February 4, 1982

XIII

LIKE FAMILY

OUR COURT, AS FAR as La Corte del Magistrado was concerned, was like a family. We were special and apart from the other court activity in Fort Smith. We were all friends. It was a traveling show. We shared stories about our family and walked to the mess hall each day for lunch. It was about two blocks away and in the old NCO club building. We even had sweatshirts with crossed Cuban and American flags announcing that we were La Corte del Magistrado. I don't believe there was another court like us—and maybe there had never been anything like us before or since. I have no idea what was done at the other relocation camps. But we felt special nonetheless.

My youngest child was born during this time on October 13, 1981. Thank God I got her in on the Federal health insurance plan! Rachael had a child about 4 years older and the same age as my son John, the streaker. We had at least one picnic for the group. Gus Saucedo, as mentioned earlier, had owned a Mexican restaurant in Eagle Pass, Texas. He brought the best guacamole I have ever tasted. We still have the recipe.

The Puerto Rican Park Police officer, Raul Jiminez, fell in love with a recently-divorced young lady. They planned to marry and live in Puerto Rico. I mentioned earlier that a child bears the name of the father and then the mother hyphenated at the end in Hispanic culture. She retained her married name in the divorce and that would be a problem. They did not want their children to be saddled with the name of her ex. I took care of that problem with a court order for a name change for her as a wedding gift. The friendships formed with the people in the system are precious to me. Judge Williams for one became a very close friend and I hurt for him when he had a stroke and had to give up his judicial duties.

My friends at the Marshals Service and the clerk's office I will never forget. Ned Stewart, Rachael Smith, Janie Gazzola and even the ever-serious-minded Neal Kirkpatrick are all special. I was blessed to be a part of it.

XIV

THE LEGACY

WHAT DID IT ALL mean? The Cubans came and they
went away. Richard Burford was right. They all wanted
to go to Miami or wherever they had family. The vast
majority ended up in Miami and very few remained in
this area. I only know of one.

Beginning in 1983, I was an Administrative Law
Judge for the Arkansas Workers Compensation Commission. One claimant that came before me had been
injured and was seeking disability. The insurance com-
pany didn't want to pay and claimed he was running a
car lot and garage from his home. They had pictures of
his house with about six cars sitting in the yard. He explained that he was one of the Cuban refugees and that
in Cuba he had not been permitted to own a car. These
were all his cars. With his accent and appearance I believed him. He won his case.

There were no lasting effects from the Mariel Boatlift in Fort Smith. The present effects had been economic
and beneficial.Several hundred people were employed.
The government spent millions of dollars on food and
supplies purchased from local merchants. Why was no
one happy about this?

I assume resentment that these multi-toned and
Spanish speaking people were intruding on their space

and disrupting their lives. Many were angry that Fidel Castro dumped many of his undesirables on our shores thanks to Cuban emigres already in Florida who financed the boatlift. Some of it was merely fear of the unknown. It was pleasing to note that when the KKK and David Duke showed up to rally opposition, only a smattering of people paid him any attention.

President Carter welcomed these desperate people to our country with open arms and that made a difference. Now we have in our country a resurgence of the KKK and the American Nazi Party and the scab has been picked from latent racism that apparently never went away. The difference is leadership. President Carter, a true Christian, believes in the tenets of Emma Lazarus' poem on the base of the Statue of Liberty:

Give me your poor, Your huddled masses yearning to breathe free, The wretched refuse of your teeming shore. Send these, the homeless, tempest-tost to me, I lift my lamp beside the golden door.

When I argued the case of Elpidio Mustelier Galan to the jury, I reminded them that the world was watching what we, The United States, was doing. They're still watching. What is it we want them to see?

JUDGE SPEARS BIOGRAPHY

JIM D. SPEARS IS a retired circuit judge who served the 12th Judicial District comprised of Sebastian County for 24 years. He previously served for 10 years as an administrative law judge for the Arkansas Workers Compensation Commission. In addition to private practice he was also an adjunct Federal Public Defender for the Cuban Relocation Project at Fort Chaffee Arkansas, from September 1980 through February 1982. He is a graduate of Westark Junior College (A.A. 1966); Arkansas Tech University (BA Hist/Pol.Sci 1968) and the University of Arkansas School of Law (JD 1973). He has had a life-long love of history and politics. He is married to the former Dixie Bean a native of Rogers, AR and they have two children and four grandchildren.

www.ingramcontent.com/pod-product-compliance
Lightning Source LLC
Chambersburg PA
CBHW071231090426

42736CB00014B/3034